PASS IT ON

CULTIVATING FUTURE GENERATIONS

By
Doris Loida Espinoza

Preface

This book has been in the making for over 30 years as God granted me opportunities in parenting and leadership. He made it crystal clear that my assignment from Him was simple—just three words: **PASS IT ON.** I found, in trying to fulfill God's assignment, that it would involve a lot of dedication and intentionality. I have learned so much from those I have trained and mentored. This reverse mentoring has been a blessing and a reward.

It's been my experience to mentor many who became my bosses, my supervisors, my leaders. What a joy to work under the supervision or leadership of one in whom I have invested so much and seen maturity, growth, creativity, and confidence. I love working under those whom God placed in my path to train and mentor. What a recompense!

I have been intentional in sharing what God has allowed me to learn, so that it extends beyond me, my family, and my generation. In reading this book, the reader has the option of just reading the content or reading and filling out reflections and questions to ponder at the end of each chapter to savor the content a little longer. For a more detailed individual or group study that can be spaced over days, weeks, or months, there are additional questions and comments to ponder, write about, or discuss individually or as a group at the back of the book.

May the content of this book give you a closer look at what matters over time and motivate you to live in such a way that you will impact your own generation and the generations that come behind you to **PASS IT ON!** Yes, what God has given you,

PASS IT ON!

About the Author

Having accepted the Lord as her Savior at the age of 11 years old, her deep desire to please God and serve Him in love and gratitude for the rest of her life grew more intense as the years passed by It was at the age of 18 that she felt God turning her life around to a new perspective in her service to Him and to new goals. She felt a call from God to make a difference and dedicate her life to ministry in service to her Lord.

Rev. Doris Loida Espinoza has been in ministry for over 54 years and has been ordained in the Assemblies of God for over 28 years. She is a graduate of Latin American Bible School (now

Christ Mission College) and of Nelson University, formerly Southwestern Assemblies of God University, with a Bachelor of Arts in Christian Education and a Master of Arts in Bible/Theology from the Harrison Graduate School at Nelson University.

At present, she is the District Girls Ministries Director of the Texas Gulf Hispanic District. She served as District Women's Ministries Sec-Treasurer for 16 years (1988–2004). She has served as District Girls Ministries Director for several years and has been part of Girls Ministries leadership, formerly Missionettes, for over 50 years.

She also serves alongside her husband, General Presbyter of the Texas Gulf Hispanic District and pastor of Templo Emanuel in Crystal City, TX—Rev. Dino Espinoza. She has served as the Missions Coordinator of mission trips all over the world for over 24 years, training Girls Ministries leaders, Women's Ministries leaders, and children's workers in several Latin American countries and other countries around the world.

She is a musician, singer, teacher, and speaker at many women's, children's, and girls' events in the United States and in foreign countries, influencing many generations. She is very active in her community and serves on the pastoral staff of Templo Emanuel, Crystal City, TX. She is Assistant Principal at Winter Garden Christian School, where she was formerly the principal and director. She is a State Certified Childcare Director and chaplain to the children/students, women, and girls of her church and community, if and as needed.

She is passionate about passing on what has been passed on to her and what God has granted her to learn through life's experiences and ministry. Doris Loida Padilla Espinoza is passionate about **"Passing it On."**

Dedication

PASS IT ON is dedicated to my family: my husband, my children and my grandchildren—spiritual and biological- who have given me every reason to write this book and put into practice and live by what it means to "PASS IT ON." My hope is that within this book you will find motivation to grasp God's personal mandate to you, regardless of your age, to PASS IT ON- Faith, the Knowledge of God, the Power of God, and the Fear of God. I have shared some treasured memories that I have used to touch other individuals and families and to prompt them to be intentional about what God expects of all of us—to PASS IT ON!

To Dina, our Treasure, you have given your Dad and me so many reasons to pursue excellence so you might grasp what that means and pursue that too. May you pass the pursuit of excellence to your children: Rosio Kiara, Sofia, Isela, Briza and Mateo. Your beautiful God-given smile enriches my life. Don't hold back on sharing that smile and telling of how God gave it to you. Your positive outlook on life and your continual reminders to others of God's grace, forgiveness, purposes and faithfulness are a blessing to many. Your music, singing, and many endeavors give us new experiences daily.

Eli, our Blessing, and Ashley, our daughter in love, your love for God, the passion with which all have sought His will, your heart-felt worship and purpose-driven ministry have prompted us to seek every way possible to witness you all flourishing wherever you are planted. Because of you, Eli, we started Rainbows for boys and girls. You also led us to start Bible Quizzing and Fine Arts. What a joy to see your children, our grandchildren-Levi and Jadon, following in your footsteps. Ashley, we can see your intentionality to Pass It On. Your family's music and singing refresh mine and your dad's spirit.

To Carlos, father of our six Roiz grandchildren. Thank you for the treasures we are blessed to share the joy and opportunity to love, teach, and mentor. You have witnessed the miraculous through what you have seen God do for you and through you. You have seen our precious grandchildren develop into dedicated servants of God. Together we will continue to make special memories. PASS IT ON- love and faith!

To our spiritual children and grandchildren all over our nation and around the world whom God has given my husband and me the opportunity to PASS IT ON, move forward in God's timing to the opportunities and doors he opens for you--mindful that as we mentored, trained, and taught you, we and God expect you PASS IT ON!

My dear husband, Dino, together we have accepted the call and assignment from God to PASS IT ON. He led us in pastoring, teaching in Bible Schools, leading and training children, youth, young adults, men and women through varied ministries. He has given us the thrill of seeing the fruit of our labor. As we grow older and move closer to being with Jesus, God continues to put persons in our path to train, love and impact. May those who come behind us find us faithful.

Sincerely

Doris Espinoza

Foreword

In her book, "**Pass It On**", Rev. Doris Loida Espinoza explains with Biblical examples our important task of instructing our youth and children as we pass the baton of service, the mantle of anointing, the shield of faith, and the torch of Pentecost. Parting from her experience as a mother and grandmother, she inspires us to take discipleship with passion and seriousness to perpetuate the faith in Christ Jesus with the next generation. Every word written by Rev. Doris Loida Espinoza is backed up by her life and testimony. I am a product of her loving and patient mentorship. Next to her husband, Rev. Dino Espinoza, she invested numerous hours instructing me to serve with excellence. And even though many of those hours were invested in working with registrations for district events and quarterly reports for the Women Ministries district and national office, nothing would start without first praying and worshipping God. Her thanksgiving praises would soon turn into intercessory prayers on behalf of the missionaries, the pastors, and especially, the women of the district. The gift that God gave her to be a composer of many songs and musical arrangements is admirable. Her children are God worshippers due to her teaching and the example seen in her and Bro. Dino. Their children have also passed the torch, and now their grandchildren are recognized by their participation at Fine Arts national competitions. Rev. Doris Loida Espinoza continues impacting others. I consider myself blessed for being part of her legacy. We are all standing on someone else's shoulders. We can see a little further in the horizon because someone is holding us. For me, it is Rev. Doris Loida and Rev. Dino Espinoza. And I am not the only one. God has given them broad and robust shoulders, for many have received their instruction, model, and above all, love. I hope this book inspires you to do precisely what its title says: "Pass It On." And as you give it all, please, keep in mind what the Psalmist says: *"Those who go out weeping, carrying seed to sow, will return with songs of joy, carrying sheaves with them."* **Psalm 126:6 (NIV)**

Maricela Hernandez

AG West Language Region Executive Presbyter

Foreword

In a world obsessed with instant gratification and fleeting trends, the timeless wisdom of mentorship often gets lost in the noise. Yet, the foundation of any enduring legacy rests not on individual brilliance, but on the deliberate act of **"passing it on."** This book, a powerful exploration of intergenerational faith and knowledge transfer, serves as a much-needed reminder of that crucial truth. Within these pages, you'll embark on a journey through the rich tapestry of biblical narratives, witnessing firsthand how pivotal figures like Paul, Elijah, and the matriarchs Lois and Eunice, understood the profound responsibility of nurturing the next generation.

Through compelling illustrations, thought-provoking challenges, and insightful analysis, the Author Doris Loida Espinoza skillfully unpacks the vital role of mentoring in preserving and perpetuating faith, values, and purpose through metaphors such as Baton of Service, Mantle of Anointing, Shield of Faith, and Torch of Pentecost. This is more than just a historical account, It is a call to action. It challenges us, the current generation, to embrace our own responsibility as mentors, as guardians of the flame. How can we ensure that the precious gifts of faith, knowledge, and experience are not lost, but are passed on, vibrant and strong, to those who will come after us? Prepare to be inspired, challenged, and equipped to embrace your vital role in shaping the future. This book is not just about the **"passing on"** of faith; it's about the **passion in the passing on**. It's about understanding that it's our turn now to leave a legacy that will resonate for generations to come. Dive in and discover the profound impact you can have.

Eddie De La Rosa

District Superintendent

TEXAS GULF HISPANIC DISTRICT

Foreword

I have known **Loida Espinoza** for many years, and I can personally testify that she is a woman who not only lives what she teaches but gives herself wholeheartedly to the calling of raising up others. Her ministry has left a mark on my life, and I can say without hesitation that part of who I am today—in ministry and in leadership—is because of people like Loida, who never hesitated to **pass it on**.

In a world where generational gaps seem wider than ever and faith is too often privatized, this book comes as a timely, Spirit-inspired call. Loida reminds us through biblical truth and personal conviction that **mentoring is God's idea**, and the responsibility to disciple, equip, and invest in the next generation belongs to all of us—not just to leaders or pastors, but to every believer who has received something worth **passing on**.

What qualifies Loida to write this book is more than her years of faithful ministry. It is the fruit of her life—the legacy of love, wisdom, and Holy Spirit empowerment she has poured into daughters and sons, both biological and spiritual. PASS IT ON is not a theory. It's a testimony, a charge, and a roadmap.

As you turn these pages, you will be stirred—not only to admire the stories of biblical mentors, but to become one yourself. This is more than a book; it's an invitation to legacy. I encourage you to read with an open heart—and be ready to act.

Let's not just be keepers of faith. Let's be **givers** of it.

Pass it on.

JR Rodriguez

Vida City Church Houston/ National Director Intercultural Ministries/Assemblies of God

Table of Content

Preface 1

About the Author 3

Dedication 5

Foreword 8

Introduction 15

Chapter 1 27

Don't Drop It - Pass It On! Importance of Mentoring 27

Chapter 2 37

Pass It On-The Baton of Service 37

Chapter 3 55

Pass It On - The Mantle of Anointing 55

Chapter 4 71

Pass It On – The SHIELD of Faith 71

Chapter 5 87

Pass It On-The Torch of Pentecost 87

Chapter 6 111

How Can This Generation Ensure Faith in God Will Be Passed On
to Future Generations? 111

Chapter 7 129

It's Our Turn 129

Selected Bibliography 151

Reflections For Deeper Individual or Group Study 152

Acknowledgements 169

A Young Generation Speaks Out 173

LIFE IS FRAGILE – God Has an Assignment—Pass it On ... 181

Introduction

Life is made up of seasons, times, and turns. Only God knows what you are going through when you pick up this book and begin reading it. Right now, you may feel like you are passing through a long, hot summer. If so, I want to encourage you that soon the cool breeze of fall—the change of weather for your life—will come.

You may feel like you are going through a dark, cold winter, but take courage, it won't always be cold and dark. Spring will come to your present situation, and you will hear birds sing and see butterflies flutter their wings as they display the lovely colors and designs the Creator has divinely painted to deliver the message of new beginnings. With spring, the flowers will bloom again, filling the air with the aroma of God's love. Look forward with faith and expect your **"New Beginning."** God's timing—for the earth with its seasons, and for our lives with the many twists, turns, and bumps—does work out for our good and to fulfill His divine purposes.

In the book of Esther, we read the following:

"And who knows whether thou art come to the kingdom for such a time as this?" (KJV)

As we read the story of Esther and the impact of her place in the palace at that specific time in history, we can see God's perfect timing and purposes unfold. I quote this verse often and have included it here to remind us that Esther had her turn to be determined and take her place. An entire nation was saved because, when it was her turn to bat, she stepped up to the plate. She hit a home run. She took her turn and did what God called her to do to ensure God's purpose in her nation—for generations to come. With prayer and fasting, she boldly declared:

"I will go to the king, even though it is against the law. And if I perish, I perish." (NIV)

As a child, I soon learned that I could not always be up to bat. I could not always be the one with the ball in my hand. Even at home, in a household of six children plus my parents, we learned very early on that we had a turn to play with certain toys, a turn to play the organ, a turn to ride the bike, and we even took turns washing dishes and doing household chores.

I am the youngest of six siblings, and it seemed my turn would never come. But it did. And maybe you thought, throughout your life, that your turn would never come—to play, to preach, to teach, to direct, or to lead—but our turn to impact the world for the Kingdom is here. Yes, it is our turn, our duty, and our privilege to play our part, to live out God's will, to walk in the miraculous through faith, and to **PASS IT ON.**

May we be mindful that it is our turn now to impact our generation and the many generations that will follow. What we say, how we live, and how we minister will make a difference in the lives of those who come behind us.

God places thoughts, truths, and ideas in our hearts that, at that moment, we have no idea of the impact they will have on our lives as time progresses. As a child, I read my name, **Loida**, on a wall at a Women's Ministries and Missionettes (name for a ministry to girls through girls' clubs) rally in Santa Fe, New Mexico. What a thrill! I had never seen my name, *Loida*, in any public place, as my name is not a common name. Now it appeared in HUGE letters, along with other girls' and ladies' names on a church wall—not only huge, but in fancy, bold letters. It was on one of the steps of a beautiful, elegant stairway that covered an entire wall. I could not believe what my eyes were seeing. It thrilled my heart! I had to find out why my name was on that wall. I am sure they did not know I was coming, and nobody there really knew me. I was accompanying my grandparents, who were Assemblies of God pastors.

I began my investigation of how and why my name was on that wall. I was informed that the Hispanic Missionettes program had the names of women in the Bible as steps to an achievement program called **"Escalera a las Estrellas."** This program, *"Stairway of the Stars,"* for girls had just begun in my church. Sister Nellie Bazan had introduced this program to the churches in Albuquerque, New Mexico. It included four steps of Bible study, each with the name of a woman in the Bible—one step for each of the first letters of the word **"STAR":**

"S" for Susanna, "T" for Tabitha, "A" for Anna, and "R" for Ruth.

I knew of this program in English; however, I was not aware that the program existed in Spanish. In Spanish, the word for "Star" is **"Estrella."** So, the Spanish program, which I was not aware existed, had eight stairs with the name of a woman of the Bible on each step. Instead of being like the English program of four steps, in Spanish there were eight steps—one name for each letter of the word **"Estrella"**:

Ester, Susana, Tabita, Rut, Eunice, Loida, Lidia, Ana.

My name, **Loida**, was one of the names of the women in the Bible. So, though my name was not one of the women's names in the English program of *Stairway of the Stars*, I was thrilled to know my name was in the Bible and that it was the name for one of the steps in this program in Spanish. Knowing this, I began a search to see who this woman, Loida, was and why her name was in the Bible.

As I inquired of the women in attendance, I was given the scripture reference of II Timothy 1:5—given to me in Spanish:

"Traigo a la memoria la fe no fingida que hay en ti, la cual habitó primero **en tu abuela Loida, y en tu madre Eunice, y estoy seguro que en ti también."** (AVCR 1959)

Translated to English, this verse reads:

"I am reminded of your sincere faith, which first lived in your grandmother **Lois and in your mother Eunice and, I am persuaded, now lives in you also."** (NIV)

Wow! I learned my name was a Spanish name, and that I had an English name now too—**Lois**. That was exciting to me! As I pondered more and searched more, I became intrigued that the woman of the Bible whom I was named after—Loida—was a grandmother whose life of faith and the transferring of that faith to her children and grandchildren was the specific reason she was mentioned in the Bible.

At that young age, I made up my mind that if I ever got married and had a baby girl, I would name her **Eunice**, and if she had a boy, I would love him to be named **Timothy** or **Timoteo**— the Spanish name for Timothy. Not knowing what it would look like or what it would mean, I also determined that if I ever became a mother or grandmother, I wanted to be a woman of faith who would pass on that faith to her children and grandchildren.

Of course, at that age, becoming a mother seemed so many, many years away—and becoming a grandmother, even more far-fetched. Yet time passed, and at the age of twenty-six, I became a mother to our first baby—a girl, **Eunice Bernardine Espinoza**, whom we lovingly call **"Dina."** My husband's name is Bernardino, and we call him "Dino" to shorten that long name. Dina's middle name was given to be the female counterpart of Bernardino—thus the nickname, "Dina." Dina is now a mother of six and a high school English Language Arts teacher who loves the Lord with all her heart. We have always called her **"Our Treasure."**

On May 31, 1984, our second child, **Eli José Espinoza**, was born. His middle name was given to him in honor of my dad, **José Leandro Padilla**. My mom's name was **Abedulia Manuelita Martinez**, who took on the last name Padilla when she married my dad. Both my parents and my husband's parents—**Bernardino Pedro Espinoza** and **Esperanza Espinoza**—along with us, welcomed our baby boy into this world, dedicating him to the Lord. We have always called him **"Our Blessing."** Eli is married to **Ashley Wright Espinoza**, a father of two sons and an ordained minister with the Assemblies of God. He is employed by

Southwest Airlines and has served in various ministries. He presently serves as the Fine Arts Coordinator of the South Central Hispanic District of the Assemblies of God.

I waited patiently and prayed that God would send us a grandson so I and my daughter, Eunice, would have a **Timothy** to whom we could pass on our faith. I wanted so much to have the opportunity to reproduce the names of three generations as they were in the Bible. But more than that, I wanted the opportunity to pass on the shield of faith—with which he could extinguish the flaming darts of the evil one, stand strong against the winds of difficulties and the temptations he would face, and experience miracles, signs, and wonders.

My daughter got married, and as her first pregnancy progressed, we began to wonder if this child in her womb was a boy or a girl. If the baby was a girl—what a thrill! But I also thought that maybe our **Timothy** could be on his way. On February 4, 2003, **Rosio Isabel Roiz** was born. We were excited and thrilled!

Within months, once again, our daughter got pregnant a second time. We would continue waiting to see if another baby girl or a baby boy would come. On May 30, 2004, our second granddaughter was born—**Kiara Anabel Roiz**. The next year, a third pregnancy came for our daughter. Another precious girl, **Sofia Miabel**, was born on June 1, 2005. My husband and I were so blessed with these bundles of joy. We poured our love and faith into their lives. What a thrill it was to see them praying and singing to the Lord! We began to think that maybe someday we would be blessed with our **Timothy**.

In 2005, our son, **Eli José Espinoza**, married **Ashley Lynaé Wright**. We prayed for them and thought that maybe we would have a grandson through them, to continue pouring our love into their children—boys or girls—as we had into our precious granddaughters. We would pass on to them the **legacy of faith**.

Our daughter got pregnant for the fourth time. On February 27, 2009, we were blessed with our daughter's fourth child, a granddaughter, **Isela Amaris Roiz**. At that time, in 2009, my son Eli and his loving wife, Ashley, were also expecting a baby. Lo and behold, on April 15, 2009, a son was born to them—our first grandson, **Levi Josiah Espinoza**—another grandchild to love, pray for, and to whom we can pass on a legacy of faith. A few years later, Eli and Ashley were blessed with a second son on March 30, 2012. They named him **Ezra Jadon Espinoza**. These two added a new and joyous dimension to our family when they joined our four granddaughters. They continue to be such a blessing.

A fifth pregnancy for our daughter, and **Briza Carina Roiz**, our fifth granddaughter, was born on September 23, 2014. Such a precious, happy baby—she brought a fresh breath of love and a gentle breeze of creativity to our family. Her Spanish name, **Briza**, translated to English, means *breeze*. I prayed to the Lord, expressing how, since I was a child, I had longed for a grandson from my daughter, Eunice. Content and so grateful for two healthy, alert, and growing grandboys from our son and our daughter-in-love, and with five beautiful, brown-eyed granddaughters from our daughter and son-in-law, **Carlos Roiz**, we praised God for His will in our family.

After five girls in a row, on September 26, 2016, our first grandson from our daughter was born. Alas, our **"Timothy"** had arrived. However, my daughter and her husband named him **Mateo**, the Spanish word for *Matthew*, which means **"Gift from God."** It rhymes so well with the Spanish name for Timothy that I call him, **"Mateo, mi Timoteo,"** which means *"Matthew, my Timothy."* He is aware of why I call him that. When I ask him, "What does that mean, and why do I call you that?" he answers, "Because I belong to God, and I am going to be a pastor and a missionary."

For God, the Bible examples of mentoring are not meant for boys only, though it happened that Eunice's offspring in the Bible was a boy, Timothy. We are responsible to pass the faith to our daughters and sons, to our grandsons and our granddaughters. I am determined to pass on to my children and grandchildren the knowledge of God and His faithfulness, the power of the name of Jesus, and the example of how the empowerment of the Holy Spirit gives us counsel, guidance, power, and discernment. I am determined to live a life in which they see the fruit of the Spirit being produced as I live out my life before their eyes.

God has put a burning passion in my heart and spirit to love and mentor not only them, but other gals, ladies, children, couples, and youth—to love and serve Him, to find their place in the Kingdom of God, and to know God's promises and experience His power in their everyday living. Their present, their future, and their eternity matter to Him, and they matter to me.

Throughout generations, a common passion to pass on valuable possessions, photos, treasured articles, impacting experiences, and skills—either naturally gifted or learned through education—has been a driving force of parents and grandparents. Families are constantly changing, prompting the need to preserve special times, special truths, special memories, and all that is highly valued so that those generations who follow can enjoy them. Each generation carries the responsibility of ensuring that highly valued articles, truths, and stories are preserved and passed on.

The challenge of taking a personal knowledge of Bible truth and a relationship with God and passing it on from generation to generation is an unending task of disciples of Jesus. What are some biblical or other examples of passing the faith from generation to generation, and how can the present generation ensure that in this age of advanced technology and compounded distractions, that faith in God will be passed on to the subsequent generations? It will, most definitely, need to be an intentional and personal goal all of us must embrace.

Rev: Tomás and Lugardita Martinez

My Maternal Grandparents

José Leandro and Abedulia Padilla

My Parents

Both couples intentionally passed on to my siblings and me love for family and faith in God.

What Does My Name Mean?

The meaning of names comes with a divine purpose. What does your name mean?

_____

_____

_____

_____

_____

_____

What has happened in your life that reflects the purpose of your name?

_____

_____

_____

_____

_____

_____

_____

My first name, Doris, was chosen because that was the name of the nurse who helped deliver me. My middle name, Loida, was suggested by my grandmother because she wanted me to have a Biblical name. I did not know that till I was older. **Have your parents ever told you why they chose that name for you**? If so, you can write it here.

_____

_____

_____

_____

_____

_____

_____

Has knowing the meaning of your name influenced your life, your goals, or what you do?

_____

_____

_____

_____

_____

_____

Chapter 1

Don't Drop It - Pass It On!
Importance of Mentoring

A story is told of a very old vase that was highly treasured by one family. It was of such special meaning and high value that it was kept on the fireplace mantle to be admired by all who came to their home. It had been handed down from generation to generation. One day, when the mother came in from shopping, her teenage daughter said, "Mother, you know that vase that has been handed down from generation to generation?"

"Yes, dear," her mother replied.

Her daughter said, "Well, this generation just dropped it."

One can imagine the devastation of parents who witness a generation dropping or disregarding something of high value that one or more generations have worked so hard to preserve and pass on. One highly valued treasure for Christian parents is faith in God. Christian parents do not want to see their children drop what they have learned, kept, practiced, experienced, and made visible for future generations.

How devastating when a generation drops the prized experience of faith in God that has been practiced and passed on generation after generation. Each generation has precious memories, commendable works, moving stories, and values it wants to pass along to the next generation. The Bible records in Psalm 145:4, "One generation commends your works to another; they tell of your mighty acts." (KJV)

Some years ago, Dr. Myles Munroe of Bahamas Faith Ministries International was interviewed on television and spoke of death on the Jeff Koinange Live Show. He so emphatically expressed the importance of mentorship and passing on to the next generation tools, helps, and living examples of faith and service to the Lord. The inspiration with which he spoke revealed the great passion he had that these be passed to the next generations, mentioning that when he died, he wanted to leave a legacy of faith and service to the Lord. He talked about emptying oneself of knowledge, experience, and talent. He said that is how he wanted to die—empty. He said his goal was that everyone dies empty. Within days, he was killed in an airplane crash, confirming that all of us have a limited time to pass on our faith in God and values. Dr. Munroe did this intentionally while he had the opportunity. He poured himself out and went to the grave empty, as desired. What a great example and legacy he left for all to follow and to help Christians realize that it is time to work at purposes and ideals like this while it is day; the night cometh, when no man can work. (John 9:4 - KJV) His last videos will live on, revealing the passion he had to mentor and empty himself till his time to leave this earth. God allowed him to accomplish his goal and inspire many. As Dr. Munroe did, let's intentionally strive to fulfill our hopes and dreams while we have the opportunity.

Consider this quote by Les Brown:

"The graveyard is the richest place on earth, because it is here that you will find all the hopes and dreams that were never fulfilled."

I want to go to the grave with my hopes and dreams to "Pass It On" fulfilled. I will do this intentionally while I have the opportunity.

The Bible gives examples of persons who intentionally mentored or shared, leaving a lasting example of godly principles and a deep faith in God. They implanted an affection for a personal relationship with God, an understanding of God's great power to perform miracles and wonders, the importance of taking God at His word, and the high price and rewards of obedience to a personal God who cares and reveals His plans. Mentoring is God's idea and plan, and He reveals that so clearly in His Word. If it is important to God, then as His children, it must be important to us. Each one of us should ask ourselves, "What am I doing to fulfill God's idea and plan to mentor someone? Have I taken the time to invest time and let someone walk beside me, behind me, and at times, when they are more knowledgeable than me in certain areas, walk ahead of me and let me learn?"

Intentionally find someone to pour into—pour your knowledge of God, His Word, and the skills and abilities He has entrusted to you. Someone needs your expertise, your love, your interest in them, and your unique personality. **PASS IT ON!**

God, through His Word, time after time relates how His servants did this and prepared workers and leaders for the Kingdom, knowing there would come a time when they would no longer be the leaders. Someone had to take their place. The Kingdom of God's agenda moves on and presses forward through those whom each generation invests in and prepares for the future.

Four such examples are:

Paul, who passed on a baton of dedicated service to **Timothy** and others;

Elijah, who passed on to **Elisha** a mantle of anointing;

Lois and **Eunice**, who passed on to **Timothy** a shield of faith;

Peter, who passed on a torch of Pentecostal Power to the **early believers**.

These persons specifically and intentionally gave of themselves not only to touch and impact specific individuals, but in touching individuals, they impacted entire generations. The examples of these persons and the passion with which they invested time, resources, knowledge, and experiences will, for generations, remind and model for others the responsibility, the joy, the energy, and the lasting impact of passing on lasting treasures to subsequent generations.

What are some lasting treasures in your family that you would like to see perpetuated in your children and your grandchildren?

_____

_____

_____

_____

What are some ideals and priorities you would like those who come behind you to uphold?

_____

_____

_____

_____

LEAVING A LASTING LEGACY: Consider Your Impact

Can you name persons who have impacted your life at different stages of your life? As a child? As a young person? As an adult?

_____

_____

_____

_____

What in their lives or in their actions made an impact on your life?

_____

_____

_____

_____

What lessons so far in your life have most impacted you?

_____

_____

_____

_____

Are you aware of something you, know, do, or share that has left/is leaving a lasting impression on others? _____ If, so, what?

_____

_____

_____

_____

What would you like future generations to remember about you?

_____

_____

_____

_____

How important is mentorship to you?

_____

_____

_____

_____

Are you willing pass on to the next generation tools, helps, and a living example of faith and service to the Lord.? What tools and helps do you want to pass on?

_____

_____

_____

_____

Are you young and desiring for someone to teach you and help you? If so, express here what it is you are wanting to learn and in what way you would like to grow.

_____

_____

_____

_____

What is it that you wish generations before you knew so they could better help or teach you?

_____

_____

_____

_____

Whatever your age, are you willing to be mentored? _____
If so, look around you, observe qualities you see in one or more persons who are impacting your life, and ask one of them if they are willing to take some time to mentor /teach you and answer some of your questions. Who might that be and why? Name those persons and the qualities you see in them.

_____

_____

_____

_____

Then take that step to let them know how they are impacting your life and pose that question. Maybe one of them will.

Pass It On
The Baton of
SERVICE

Chapter 2

Pass It On-The Baton of Service

Paul was an apostle of the Lord Jesus Christ, who had persecuted Christians. After a transforming experience on the road to Damascus, Paul was changed into a determined and dedicated servant of the Lord. He was a chosen instrument by God to proclaim Christ's name to the Gentiles. Throughout his ministry, Paul was used by God in the working of miracles. God used him mightily as a preacher, teacher, and missionary. The book of Acts and the epistles Paul wrote describe the many challenges that Paul faced and the victories he won.

Paul was educated, skilled, gifted, and devoted. His vision beyond his own generation led him to seek out and train young workers who were strong, to ensure that what he lived, preached, and taught would be passed on. One of those young workers was Timothy. His letters reveal how important the passing on of sound teaching and dedication to God's standards were to him, and how he wanted to leave that imprinted on Timothy and all those with whom he came into contact throughout his ministry and before God called him home.

It is in Acts 16:1–3 that Timothy begins his spiritual journey, or race. The Bible reveals that his mother was Jewish, and his father was Greek. Timothy's mother and grandmother were believers. Scripture gives no indication that his father was a believer. Verse 3 records that Paul chose Timothy to go with him and had him circumcised because of the Jews, for they knew that his father was a Greek.

Timothy becomes a companion in travels and ministry. He also becomes an official representative for Paul in regions, cities, and churches where Paul could not go. We read how Paul uses athletic illustrations in his writings and teaches Timothy to run the race to win. In 1 Corinthians 9:24, Paul expresses the following:

"Do you not know that in a race all the runners run, but only one gets the prize? Run in such a way as to get the prize." (NIV)

Paul likens the journey of faith to a race that must be run with diligence, caution, and endurance. Along this race, there are highs and lows—difficulties and victories. He teaches Timothy how to run this race with patience, confidence, and faith in God.

In Philippians 2:19–22, Paul writes of the high esteem he has for Timothy. He had full confidence in Timothy's love and passion for those who worked in the various churches, and he compares their ministry relationship to that of a father and son, as Timothy served with him in the gospel. Though Paul had many companions and mentored many, he mentions Timothy more than any other. Though he was much younger than Paul, he was willing to leave his own home to accompany him. On many trips, they encountered dangers and difficulties, but Timothy remained faithful. Perhaps the knowledge that Paul regularly practiced praying in the Spirit and with understanding, as well as knowing Paul prayed for him continuously and mentioned it in his letters, gave Timothy the boost, the motivation, and the drive to press on. At Paul's side, Timothy experienced the challenges, sufferings, and hardships, but also got a taste of the triumphs and victories God granted Paul!

Paul was passing on the baton of service as he included Timothy in his ministerial opportunities. What an impressive joint ministry of two generations they experienced. We read about them in the Pauline letters—a model for us.

In 1 Thessalonians 3:1–2, Timothy is sent to Thessalonica to strengthen the brothers there. At Corinth, Timothy worked with Paul and accompanied him when he returned to Macedonia. We read how he was in close contact with Paul during his first imprisonment in Rome.

There was a time when the Apostle Paul was expected to be released from jail shortly, and in Philippians 2:19 he wrote that he expected to send Timothy. Later, Timothy goes to Ephesus. While there, Timothy receives a letter from Paul urging him to come to him in Rome. Paul indicates that he is facing death. In 2 Timothy 4:7, Paul concludes his metaphor of life being a race and now points Timothy and us to finishing the race with some special words of direction and encouragement:

"But watch thou in all things, endure afflictions, do the work of an evangelist, make full proof of thy ministry. For I am now ready to be offered, and the time of my departure is at

hand. I have fought a good fight, I have finished my course (my race), I have kept the faith: Henceforth there is laid up for me a crown of righteousness, which the Lord, the righteous judge, shall give me at that day: and not to me only, but unto all them also that love his appearing. Do thy diligence to come shortly unto me." (KJV)

The Bible does not say if Timothy ever got there, but what a mentor Paul was. To the very end, he guides and works to ensure that his young partner goes forth in valor, and Paul finishes the race. He modeled for us what it is to **PASS ON the BATON of SERVICE**. How important it is not only to begin a race but to finish the race. Paul is a great example of taking time to prepare a successor, ensuring that faith in the living God is passed on. Paul was faithful to pass on to Timothy the baton of dedicated service. Timothy goes on to a life of dedicated service to God and to the people of God.

Every Christian has a baton—a spiritual inheritance in Christ—which is worth passing on. There is always someone coming behind us who can glean from what God has done and is doing in us. Our baton is the sum of the lessons learned, the wisdom God has given, the insights God has granted us, plus the spiritual anointing God has poured upon us. Our baton is the spiritual legacy God wants us to impart to others. The passing on of the baton to the generations that come behind us will encourage, inspire, and empower them.

I have, throughout my life and ministry, attempted to include children and young people in what I do for the Lord. One of the young gals from our church who grew up in our church and then went off to Bible college to pursue God's call on her life was Cassie Mata.

Cassie agreed to be held accountable, and I asked her questions about every month or two. We would have a conversation over her goals, her fears, her ministry. I listened. Sometimes it was at church, sometimes it was at my dining room table. Sometimes she and I were so busy, we would meet at the track or a walking trail and take advantage of those times of exercise to talk.

A lot of passing the baton may be taking place, but if nobody is taking the baton and continuing the race, the race is over. It is lost, and we all lose. I thank God for Cassie, and I thank Cassie for that desire to take the baton. There is a special anointing on her life, and like Timothy, may Cassie and others who have walked beside me through years of youth work, pastoring, education at our Christian school/daycare, missions trips, and years of work in Women's Ministries and Girls Ministries, take the baton of service. My heart has been to give to those who walk beside me and to those from the generations behind me everything I can of what God and others have passed on to me.

Another young minister who walked beside me very closely is Maricela Hernandez. Serving in a district position, I spoke with many gals in ministry and asked them to come help me in the ministry I was working in, which at that time was Women's Ministries of the Gulf Latin American District Council. Of the many to whom I opened this opportunity, only two responded: Rev. Rosita Cantu and Rev. Maricela Hernandez. They helped me so much in preparation for big events with over 700 ladies in attendance at camps and conventions, which later climbed to over 1,000 ladies. As they came to help, I would teach them what I had learned through my years of experience and through ladies such as Gloria Garza, my mentor in the work of Girls Ministries and Women's Ministries. Sister Maricela continued working with me, and Sister Rosita went on to teach at our Christ Mission College (then Latin American Bible Institute), and later went on to work in Springfield, Missouri. She earned her Doctorate Degree at Assemblies of God Theological Seminary.

Through approximately eight years of working together, Maricela and I became an effective working team to serve our district, along with and under the anointed leadership of Rev. Gloria Garza. Sister Gloria Garza had knowledge, experience, and a fragrance of grace and beauty. She gave us freedom to use our creativity for Girls Ministries and Women's Ministries. She encouraged us to pursue excellence in all we did. I will forever be grateful for the impact of Gloria Garza's life on my life and ministry. She lovingly taught me by example what a good leader is and does. She gave over 40 years of her life to lead in Girls Ministries and Women's Ministries. I think of her often as I minister and thank God that He gave me such a wise woman and such a dedicated servant to be my mentor. Both Sister Maricela and I gleaned from her anointed leadership.

In between or on breaks during those weeks when Maricela would come to help me, we would share sermons or insights God would give us on different Bible verses. We built a long-lasting friendship so close that she became like a daughter. I can relate with Paul and Timothy becoming like a father/son relationship. She learned how to organize and fulfill office duties, how to prepare and load up supplies and materials for our events, and would even miss out on the last hour or two of some events to help me prepare and load up as the events were ending. It was a lot of sacrifice to drive 4–5 hours and spend 2 or 3 days here at my home to help me in our WM District Office adjacent to my home, but it proved her love for the Lord, her desire to help, and her love for learning to serve in many areas of Kingdom work. Prayer times together and sharing our thoughts and lessons in life were always the highlight of her trips here.

Only God and we knew the long working hours we put into preparing our events with excellence so that everything was organized, so that registration and the program would run smoothly, and so the theme of the events would be engraved in the ladies' hearts. We wanted God to work in us and in the ladies to refresh and empower us at each event for what lay ahead for each one of us.

After a few years, I was no longer teaching Sister Maricela, but she became my leader as the Director of the Women's Ministries of our district—Gulf Latin American District. Later, she was elected the Secretary-Treasurer of our conference and then of our new district, Texas Gulf Hispanic District. My husband was elected Superintendent of our conference first, then of our new district, and she served as the Secretary-Treasurer during the terms he served in that ministry. She was an excellent Secretary-Treasurer in those years she served (approximately eight years), with Rev. Eddie De La Rosa serving as our Assistant District Superintendent then. The three of them worked as a team to lead our district in its initial launch with great strides in church planting and in missions giving, as they ministered to the churches and ministers of our district.

Little did I know when I was teaching and mentoring her that we would reap the benefits of what she learned as she so efficiently served under my husband's leadership. Pastor Eddie also worked so closely with my husband, fulfilling so diligently all the tasks my husband would assign to him in the district. His excellence in fulfilling tasks assigned gained him God's favor, our favor, and the favor of our district. He was later elected as our District

Superintendent and presently serves in that capacity today. Bro. Eddie De La Rosa and Sister Maricela worked alongside my husband and me for many years. Then the time came that they became our bosses, our leaders. Sister Maricela continues to serve with excellence as Secretary-Treasurer of our district, while our Assistant Superintendent, Rev. Rick Reyes, completes this outstanding executive team. Together, they have taken—and are taking—our district to new heights in so many areas. How thankful we are for these and other leaders we have mentored.

Sister Maricela Hernandez has gone on to become a church planter and has been awarded national recognition in that area. She was also elected to serve on the Executive Presbytery of the General Council of the Assemblies of God as one of the first Hispanic women elected to that decision-making body of the Assemblies of God.

In 2016, at the age of 65, I earned my master's degree in Bible and Theology. She was one of the first to tell me, "You have set an example for the rest of us." In May of 2021, she earned her master's degree in Ministry Leadership at the Assemblies of God Theological Seminary. I am proud of her and have been blessed to play a small part in what God has done and continues to do through this dynamic vessel who is touching our lives and the lives of so many through her extensive ministry. What a blessing she is to us and to our district.

One thing I can say about Sister Maricela is that she frequently and publicly thanks me—acknowledging me as her mentor at the events where she speaks.

We never know where God will take those we pour into. Let's just give them the best we know, share with them our knowledge, our experiences, our life—and let them learn. It could be that they will become our leaders or bosses. Let's not see this as a fear, but as a reward from God. God bless our mentors, and God bless those who are willing to be mentored and taught. They and we will reap a harvest if we don't give up (Galatians 6:9).

I was blessed as a small girl in Sunday School at Aposento Alto in Albuquerque, New Mexico (now Casa del Rey), with women like Sister Sofia Chavez and Sister María Martinez—Sunday School teachers—and with Sister Florence Trujillo, my Missionettes Girls Club sponsor. In my teen years, I was mentored by Sister Susie Jaramillo, my Sunday School teacher, and by my youth leaders, who in the '60s were Richard and Corene Espinoza, and Johnny and Jenny Baca. I saw their dedicated service to make everything attractive for us to want to be in church, and I witnessed their love for the Word of God. They not only taught God's Word, but they lived out God's Word as we saw them weekly in class and in other activities throughout the week.

I was inspired and learned so much from the staff at Latin American Bible Institute: Sister Cuquita Martinez, Sister Abigail Arauza, Sister Eileen Cisneros, Sister Elaine Duran, Sister Edna Villarreal, and Sister Marylou Vega. My cousin, Mary Padilla, taught me so much on prayer and on missions trips. I am who I am today, and I do what I do, because of the input of these persons in my life: my pastors—Rev. Fidel and Belle Martinez, Rev. Antonio and Sister Josephine Enriquez, Rev. Jose and Sister Hilaria Salazar, Rev. Nestor and Sister Celia Bazan, and Rev. Ruben and Sister Hortencia Guajardo.

I was blessed in the year 2010 to preach in Dallas, Texas, for the National Women in Ministry Conference. At that time, I was serving as the National Representative of all the Hispanic Women in Ministry on the National Women in Ministry Taskforce of the Assemblies of God, under the leadership of Dr. Beth Grant.

As we met to plan the Women in Ministry Conference in Dallas for 2010, we were asked to suggest persons whom we thought would be a good choice for a speaker for that event. We all gave names. At that time, I recommended Evelyn Klinger, a friend whom I respect and love the way God uses in the preaching of the Word. Many on the taskforce gave their suggestions. To my surprise, Beth Grant recommended me. I was shocked, surprised, and was somewhat trembling. She had only heard me speak the night before in a devotional I gave the taskforce upon her request. Somehow a vote was taken, and before I knew it, I was selected to be one of the speakers.

I was humbled to be selected as a speaker at a national event, and I went through questions in my own mind like: *Why me? Would I be able to deliver what they were expecting of a speaker?* There are so many dynamic speakers they could have selected.

God, by His Spirit, tenderly reminded me of a Bible verse I had quoted so many times, and one I continue to declare almost daily. As my mind was racing with so many questions and fears of meeting the expectations for the National Women in Ministry Conference to be held in Dallas, Texas in October of 2010, God brought that verse to my memory. It kept repeating in my mind and began to be absorbed by my spirit:

"The steps of the righteous are ordered by God." (Psalm 37:23)

When I have quoted this verse, my mind pictures steppingstones leading up to a beautiful home. I imagine how God has already placed the steppingstones that we are to step on as we make our way toward our eternal home. If I carefully step on those stones in the positions and the pattern in which they have been placed, I will fulfill God's purpose for my life here on earth and make it to the eternal home He has prepared for me.

As I sought the Lord about what I would share at that Women in Ministry Conference, the very title of this book was the title of the message God gave me to share at that conference, **"PASS IT ON."** A few years later, I felt a nudge from the Lord to write a book to include a lot of what God had given me for that conference to encourage and challenge all God's children to consider that what God has given us is not to be kept within the perimeters of comfort and what we can see, but to be shared to impact the generations that come behind us.

I remember how God uniquely guided me as I prepared to deliver that message for the Women in Ministry Conference. I felt led to close that message with a girl, young gal, or lady from each decade. I had one of my granddaughters represent the decade of 1–10 years old, a young lady from our Bible school represent the decade of 11–20 years old, a gal representing the decade of 21–30 years old, a partner in ministry representing the decade of 31–40, and so on—respectively for every subsequent generation that follows—so that we had one for each decade up to the decade of 81–90 years old.

What a victory in the Kingdom of God as I spoke and as those attending saw the representation of the decades and the importance that all decades hear of and know the power of God. It was, most definitely, inspiring to see all the decades represented and those born in those decades embrace the importance of passing on to the generations behind us the virtues of our spiritual heritage.

Let us pass on a living example of dedication to serve, and release the baton of service to them for what God has called them to do—when and as God guides.

Men, let those young boys and men walk beside you as you serve and carry out the ministries God has called you to fulfill or as you serve others in your professions.

Ladies, let's take the teen gals, the young ladies, and women on missions trips, on ministry outreaches, and to conferences, so they may experience the miraculous, learn about spiritual warfare, and know the hope to which God has called them. Let's invite them to volunteer and help in camps, conventions, and events. In your professions, include them in various areas they can help, thus exposing them to service in varied ways.

We are preparing them to be leaders, and when we transition in ministry or professions, are older and cannot do the work anymore—or are gone—they will be ready to step in and take their turn, because they were taught as they did the many duties and as they fulfilled the many responsibilities that ministries for the Lord and for other professions entail.

As they see life and ministry modeled for them by the previous generations, their hearts will be moved, and their spirits ignited to follow in our footsteps.

I remember a missions trip I directed to Honduras, a country in Central America, in which, again, I felt the Holy Spirit nudge me to take a girl, young gal, or woman whose age would represent each decade, as far as I could. It was so important to God to ensure that there would be no gap in the fulfilling of the Great Commission. As God was leading me to this, I told the Lord in my prayers for this trip that He would be the one to call out and provide one gal from each decade. I announced what God was leading me to do and what decades still had no representative. The Lord was faithful! He called out the gals of the decades we were missing and provided, so that we had one from each decade on the trip—up to the decade of the 80–90-year-olds.

One experience during this trip that I cannot forget is that we did not have a gal to represent the decade of the 10–20-year-olds. After much prayer and fasting, asking God to call out the last team member needed to fulfill what He had asked me to do, a young lady, Liz Burgos, finally called to let me know she felt God had called her to be the representative of that decade.

As we began to plan and try booking her flight, I was told that the plane fares the rest of us had gotten had shot up to over $1,000. The rest of us had paid from $350 to $500, depending on when we purchased and paid for our tickets. I told the attendant who was trying to book the flight that, just yesterday I had checked, and it was $480. She told me to book it now because it was only going to go higher.

This precious gal could not afford to pay over $1,000. I told the attendant, "I will wait and pray." Her words to me were: "You can pray all you want to, but it's only going to get higher if you try later."

I thought to myself, *"Who is she to tell me that my God cannot make this happen?"*

I hung up, called the young lady, and several others on the team to help me pray—we needed a miracle.

Later that evening, I called back, trusting God would miraculously work to bring that flight fare down. Interestingly, it was the same gal. I inquired about the fare while in my heart I was praying and trusting. She told me, "Ma'am, I told you it would only go higher. Now it is $1,350." I hesitated and just thought a prayer in my head and trusted in God with all my heart. I knew other team members were praying too.

Then suddenly she said, "Wait a minute. I don't know what is happening. Right before my eyes, I see the flight appearing for below $500. This never happens."

I told her, "Book it."

It was an amazing, memorable missions trip with many miracles. We all experienced the supernatural, learned so much about that culture, and learned that it will take some sacrifice for all of us to give up some conveniences for the sake of the call to fulfill the Great Commission. We also learned about the joy, the reward, and the fulfillment that comes with giving God our time, money, and talent to fulfill the command Christ left for us: to go tell the good news to the world and make disciples.

To this day, many of those gals continue to accompany me on other missions trips. They caught it because we took them by the hand and walked it with them—not just because they read about it.

Paul leads Timothy on a race wherein he passes him the baton of service, admonishing him to do his best to present himself to God as one approved, a worker who has no need to be ashamed, rightly handling the word of truth (2 Timothy 2:15), and calls for him as he is finishing his race.

Paul impacted entire regions and handed down a baton of powerful service and missionary vision.

May we be inspired to do what Paul modeled for us and PASS IT ON—the BATON of SERVICE.

Passing the baton is an act of entrusting someone else with a particular duty or function, allowing them to take over and continue the work or task. Are you willing to serve in such a way that it impacts others and leaves an imprint on their lives that will inspire them to take the baton of service you have modeled for them? How can you accomplish this?

_____

_____

_____

_____

_____

What areas of service are you serving in? Are you sharing with those younger than you how to best serve in that area?

_____

_____

_____

_____

Once you release it, can you allow them to "run" in their own way and be supportive?

_____

_____

_____

_____

_____

Has someone ever passed a baton of service on to you? If so, whom, and how?

List more than one if applicable.

_____

_____

_____

_____

_____

_____

Try to articulate what baton of service you project passing on to others.

_____

_____

_____

_____

_____

_____

Pass It On - The MANTLE Of ANOINTING

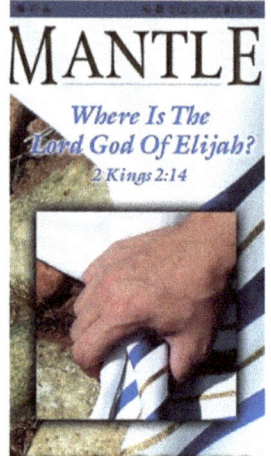

Chapter 3

Pass It On - The Mantle of Anointing

Elijah was a well-known prophet whose story begins in **1 Kings 17:1**. The Bible records that Elijah prophesied to King Ahab about an upcoming drought to be broken only, "by my word," as Elijah told the king. The Lord led Elijah to a brook, and there the ravens brought food to Elijah morning and evening—until the brook dried up. Then we read in Elijah's story that he is fed by a widow in Zarephath, and God later uses Elijah to restore life to the widow's son when he dies. God uses the prophet and works miracles through the word given by God to this man.

After years of service to God as a prophet, Elijah journeys to Abelmeholah as the Lord had commanded him. There, in a large farming field owned by Shaphat, Elijah walks until he reaches

Shaphat's son. There, he unfastens his mantle and places it on the young man—Elisha. God had chosen Elisha to be a prophet who was to follow the older prophet and help him in every way. I love reading how the young Elisha was ready to obey. Here begins a model of mentorship—a marvelous partnership in ministry: of the old teaching the young, the passing on of faith for another generation, and the younger generation experiencing the power of God to do miracles. Through this faith walk, the future generation was learning the significance of walking with God in obedience and exercising faith and confidence in an all-powerful God.

Elisha, the young man, leaves his father's farm and becomes a prophet-in-training as Elijah's attendant and companion. Elijah serves God for many years, and in **2 Kings 2:9**, the Bible records that Elijah's time of departure is near:

"And it came to pass, when they were gone over, that Elijah said unto Elisha, 'Ask what I shall do for thee, before I be taken away from thee.' And Elisha said, 'I pray thee, let a double portion of thy spirit be upon me.' And he said, 'Thou hast asked a hard thing: nevertheless, if thou see me when I am taken from thee, it shall be so unto thee; but if not, it shall not be so.'" (KJV)

After these words are spoken by Elijah, Elisha walks faithfully and steadfastly with his master, not wanting to miss the moment of his departure—and the answer to the request he has expressed.

In Bible times, a man's eldest son always inherited a double share of his wealth. This was a sign that he was his father's successor. Elisha longs to be his master's successor. The Bible describes that a blazing chariot appears, drawn by horses of fire. Elijah mounts the chariot and is taken to heaven in a whirlwind. Elisha gets to be an eyewitness, and soon after, he sees Elijah's mantle fall to the ground.

"He took up the mantle of Elijah that fell from him, and went back, and stood by the bank of Jordan; and he took the mantle of Elijah that fell from him, and smote the waters, and said, 'Where is the Lord God of Elijah?' And when he also had smitten the waters, they parted hither and thither: and Elisha went over." (2 Kings 2:13–14, KJV)

The time, knowledge, and experience of Elijah's life and ministry were shared with the young Elisha. The desire for a spiritual treasure over material possessions was provoked in the young man through consistent companionship. The visible answer to Elisha's plea and desire for a double portion of his spirit ensured that living faith, a prophet, and a knowledge of God's power were alive for the generation after Elijah. Elijah empowered his successor to continue the race he began. He understood the truth that man has a limited time to **pass it on**.

I remember so vividly the year **1985**. We had accepted a pastorate in Crystal City, Texas, after **12 ½ years** of leading the youth of the Gulf Latin American District of the Assemblies of God (GLAD). My husband was the District Christ Ambassadors President (DCAP). From 1973–1985, my husband, Rev. Dino Espinoza, led the youth in our district. We were so active—training and mentoring youth leaders all over the district, planning camps and singles retreats.

As he planned those events along with his officers, he was sharing all he had learned about contracts with campgrounds and hotels, planning the programs, seeking out speakers, and all that planning events entails. But more importantly, he was teaching them that **prayer is the key** to the success of any event or endeavor that brings youth, leaders, and parents together for a refreshing, empowering experience. Like Elijah, he was pouring into his officers and area leaders. He was passing on that mantle of anointing.

The first officers that served with him were Rev. James Plata as Vice President and Rev. Teodoro Gonzalez as Secretary-Treasurer. Later, Rev. Raymond Martinez, Rev. Sam Lopez, and Rev. Rick Gonzalez were elected to serve in this district youth ministry.

My husband felt led of the Lord to begin youth conventions. We had never had one before, so the GLAD District Superintendent at that time, Dr. Josué Sanchez, had many questions for him—how he thought it would be financed, and other pertinent concerns. Finally, he approved my husband, as District Youth President, to plan and prepare for the first youth convention for our district. That year, it was held in **San Antonio, Texas**, in **December of 1973** during the Christmas vacation of our students. The attendance was a little over **700**.

By the next year, the date of the youth convention was changed to **Thanksgiving weekend**, when all students are also off from school.

Each year, the Christ Ambassadors Youth Convention would increase in attendees. This called for preparing more workers and leaders. It required the delegation of many duties that a convention includes and mentoring those who would be leading in future years. By the time we left Youth Ministries in 1985 to take the pastorate in Crystal City, attendance at our annual youth convention had grown from a little over 700 to a little over 4,000. **All glory to God!** God had opened doors, given favor, and the youth leaders and youth pastors were rising to the challenge that the growth demanded.

My husband led and mentored young men who served as his officers, and when he left—**in God's timing**—to take the pastorate in Crystal City, the leaders that followed grew the GLAD Youth Convention to about 8,000 youth. Many were being saved, delivered from addictions, baptized in the Holy Spirit, encouraged, restored, and called to ministry. Other District Christ Ambassadors Presidents (DCAPs)—whose title later changed to District Youth Directors (DYDs)—who served after him were Rev. Moses Cavazos, Rev. J. R. Rodriguez, Rev. Charlie Rivera, and Rev. Mike Fernandez.

My husband and all these leaders were faithful to train and prepare their successors. The mantle of anointing was **intentionally** passed on to ensure that Youth Ministries would always have an anointed leader ready and equipped to serve. All these men were gifted and educated. They could have held high positions in the secular world, but the call on their lives and their passion to see youth experience a move of God and pursue God's purpose led them to take that mantle of anointing when it was their turn. They served God and our district youth with excellence.

A big **thank you** to each of these Youth Presidents/Directors and their families for saying, **"Yes, Lord."** Our district experienced and witnessed the anointing on each of those leaders as they took their turn to lead. Our Bible colleges have students in training, our churches have pastors and missionaries on the field, and our ministries have district and national leaders—**because these men were faithful to pass on the mantle of anointing**. Like Elijah, they were not afraid to pass on their knowledge, their experience, and their passion—their mantle of anointing.

Since then, the Gulf Latin American District of the Assemblies of God restructured to meet the growth in the number of churches and the distance required to travel to district events. Four districts were formed from the one, and each continued to hold their youth conventions. Faithful leaders continued to pass the mantle of anointing.

Last year—**2024**—marked **50 years** since my husband held the first youth convention. He has **not missed** a single youth convention. How important it is to be supportive and attend events one has invested in and pioneered, even when one is no longer the one in charge or on the stage.

Amazingly, the year 2024 was a year of **great celebration** because those dedicated youth leaders in our district were faithful to pass on the mantle of anointing. They were willing to invest in the young leaders coming up, until they learned the skills and had the spiritual maturity to take their turn. In that year (2024), the youth of all four districts came together in a historic celebration—a **united youth convention** in Dallas, Texas.

What wonders can be perpetuated when leaders are willing to mentor and pass on the mantle of anointing!

My husband—lovingly called by all, **Bro. Dino**—like Elijah, empowered his successors to continue the race, serve with diligence, and carry on what was begun. Youth leaders continued planning ministries and events Youth Ministries had started. They understood the truth that **each of us has a limited time to pass it on**. Let us never forget that important truth, and let us take advantage of the days God gives us.

Yes, the story of Elijah and Elisha is an example from the Old Testament about **mentorship that produces hope and help** for the next generation. By transferring what he knew, what he had experienced, and what God could do, Elijah did not decrease in impact or compromise his legacy. On the contrary, he **ensured and enabled** his ministry as a prophet to continue for another generation. We read how it even **doubled** in impact through Elisha.

Perhaps some may think that they will compromise their position, title, or legacy if they transfer and share their knowledge and experience with the next generation. May we all take heed to **share and transfer to those behind us a legacy of ministry, service, and knowledge of the power of God.**

God continues to raise up **Elijahs** and **Elishas** to carry on His Kingdom work.

The question for each one of us is:

Will we be Elijahs and Elishas?

We **can be mentors**, passing on what we have learned and experienced to someone to prepare them to serve.

We **can also be mentees**, learning from someone to do the work God may call us to.

Mike Fernandez, Charlie Rivera, J.R. Rodriguez, Moses Cavazos, Dino Espinoza

The 5 District Directors of Gulf Latin American District Council who led Youth Conventions-
They PASSED ON THE MANTLE OF ANOINTING!

Mike Fernandez honored his four predecessors at one of the youth conventions he led. How crucial and important it is that we recognize and honor those who have had a part in preparing the way for us to lead.

Just as the example of **Paul and Timothy** in the New Testament revealed to us the **passing on the baton of service**, this example from the Old Testament—of **Elijah passing on to Elisha the mantle of anointing**—ensured that faith in and obedience to God was passed on.

We also have some young people—**men and women** in these days—who serve as wonderful examples of **passing on their giftings and ministries** to the generations behind them.

Let us **pass on to those who come behind us** the mantle of anointing God has entrusted to us.

Are we being faithful as they were or are being? You are the only one who can answer that question? Ponder on this question, then write your answer below.

Are you being faithful in passing on the mantle of anointing in the areas of leadership that God has gifted and anointed you?

_____

_____

_____

_____

_____

If so, how?

_____

_____

_____

_____

_____

If not, try starting today. What God has gifted you in will benefit and prepare others for their service to God. Can you think of someone you could share your gifts with and invest in? List them:

_____

_____

_____

_____

_____

What areas of ministry and what giftings are you sharing/teaching or could you share or teach for others to learn and repeat in their own way with the flair of their personal touch as God gifts and anoints them for their own time?

_____

_____

_____

_____

_____

There are various meanings of mantle in the Bible, but the most common and main idea is that of a covering such as a cloak, robe, or other article of clothing. The mantle was a covering. How has God covered you?

_____

_____

_____

Another meaning of mantle is anointing. How has God anointed you?

_____

_____

_____

Have you at any time seen a vessel of God and thought, "I would like his/her mantle to fall on me. If so, whom? and why?

_____

_____

_____

I had a woman of grace, strength, and beauty, Rev. Gloria Garza, who believed in me. She taught me, trained me, and prepared me to lead in Girls Ministries and Women's Ministries. She taught with patience, led by example, and inspired me with her passion and dedication. She was not afraid to release me to do new things they had never done before. If I made a mistake, she lovingly let me know better ways to do things. I had known her before I worked with her and had looked up to her as a leader, and thought, "I would like her mantle to fall on me." I never imagined God would grant me the privilege of working with her and under her leadership. Like Elijah, she wisely and lovingly passed on the mantle of anointing. I am still leading in Girls Ministries as of the writing of this book. I know I am and have been mentoring and preparing, possible successors, and very soon I will be passing on the mantle. What stage of ministry or life are you in right now? Are you mentoring/preparing successors who will be ready to take the mantle, or are you in training to be ready to take the mantle of anointing when God, in his timing allows it. It could be both as God transitions you to other phases or stages of life, in your profession or your ministry.

_____

_____

_____

_____

_____

_____

_____

Can you truly say you have the desire for a spiritual treasure over material possessions as Elisha did? _____ If so, what has provoked that desire in your life?

_____

_____

_____

Elijah and Elisha's story leaves a great example of passing a mantle of anointing. Write your thoughts or reflection on your initial impression or take on this biblical account.

_____

_____

_____

Let us pass on to those who come behind us the examples of love and devotion for God, the mantle of anointing God has entrusted to us as we follow his instructions and are used by Him.

Another one of my partners in ministry alongside Gloria Garza was Gloria Bocanegra Ramos. Though we are the same age, her love for winning souls, her passion to worship God, and her example as a dedicated prayer warrior impacted my life and the lives of girls and women God called us to lead as a team. Be specific and name someone or several persons and what about them has impacted you.

_____

_____

_____

_____

_____

As our district, the Gulf Latin American District, transitioned to the four districts, I worked on a team of anointed women to lead that transtion and prepare the new four districts in the making. We trained and prepared leaders who would lead the new districts in Girls Ministries and Womens Ministries. I was blessed to work with Sister Marylou Madrigal as District Director of Women's Ministries, with Sister Saraí Luna as Secretary-Treasurer. I was elected to serve as the Assistant District Women's Ministries Director with the dual role of District Girls Ministries Director. Sister Janie Gonzalez was appointed to assist me in Girls Ministries .

That was 2008-2010. Interestingly, as of this year, 2025, I am leading Girls Ministries in our district, and the gal who assisted me 15 years ago, is now once again assisting me in this ministry. God has so many ways of surprising us. Both of us love what we do!

In those 2 years we worked hard-training, preparing every Girls Ministries and Womens Ministries leader to take her place in leadership in the new districts. I learned so much from these ladies. They were filled with wisdom, knowledge, and I could tell they all had an intimate relationship with God. I grew and they grew. Now as we see the four districts flourishing in these ministries, we thank God and have a deep sense of fulfillment, knowing God had called us for that time to prepare the districts. We all continue to serve in pastorates or other ministries, but we will cherish those two years (2008-2010) God gave us to prepare for what was to come.

I had been in these ministries for many years, so I know they learned much from me, but I also learned so much from them. What was so beautiful is how we gleaned and learned from each other. Have you had the opportunity to work in a team at work, at school, or in ministry? Could you take the time here to name one or many of those team members you trained and/or learned from and the qualities that impacted you as you worked on that or those teams. Feel free to elaborate as God brings to your memory some of those precious/surprising/challenging experiences or difficult decisions you faced.

_____

_____

_____

_____

_____

_____

I am reminded of your sincere faith, which first lived in your grandmother Lois and in your mother Eunice and, I am persuaded, now lives in you also. II Timothy 1:5(NIV)

Pass On
The

SHIELD of FAITH

Finally, be strong in the Lord and in his mighty power. Put on the full armor of God, so that you can take your stand against the devils's schemes. …take up the shield of faith with which you can extinguish the flaming arrows(fiery darts) of the evil one. (Ephesians 6: 1, 16)

Chapter 4

Pass It On – The SHIELD of Faith

The Bible also highlights a mother and grandmother, **Eunice and Lois**, who diligently invested time to pass on the **shield of faith**. Lois and Eunice (Timothy's grandmother and mother) leave a long-lasting model of how to pass down faith in a living God to children and grandchildren.

It is not clear exactly when Timothy's family became Christian, but Scripture reveals that Timothy grew and matured in his faith under the spiritual guidance of these dedicated ladies. From the days of his childhood, Timothy was instructed in the sacred writings of the Old Testament. So, even before he was mentored by Paul, Timothy was taught, trained, and fed a steady and spiritually nourishing foundation of steadfast and enduring faith at home by his mother and grandmother.

Paul mentions this in **2 Timothy 1:5**:

"When I call to remembrance the unfeigned (sincere) faith that is in thee, which dwelt first in thy grandmother Lois, and thy mother Eunice; and I am persuaded that in thee also." (KJV)

What a solid foundation these two women laid for Timothy. They prepared him for service in God's Kingdom. He flourished from the instruction at home, learned and served at the side of an apostle, and then rose to the challenge after his mentor was gone.

Though the Bible mentions these women in only one verse, they shine as **outstanding testimonies** and **role models** for me and for others—far beyond their generation—of what instructing one's children and grandchildren can produce for the family and for God's Kingdom.

The Bible so emphatically instructs God's children to teach their children and grandchildren about faith in God:

"Only take heed to thyself, and keep thy soul diligently, lest thou forget the things which thine eyes have seen, and lest they depart from thy heart all the days of thy life: but teach them to thy sons, and thy sons' sons." (Deuteronomy 4:9, KJV)

It is of **utmost importance** that parents and grandparents be intentional about passing down faith to their children and grandchildren. The Bible talks about faith as a **shield** with which they will extinguish the fiery darts of the enemy (Ephesians 6).

Lois and Eunice, by passing on the shield of faith to Timothy, were ensuring that he would have protection from the philosophies and crooked ways of thinking of that day.

In this crucial time in history, with its many distractions, we cannot just tell children what to do in the way of service, devotion, and faithfulness to God. **Parents must model it for them.** This generation is crying out, *"Don't tell me—show me."* It is evident that Lois and Eunice not only taught the Scriptures, but were **faith-driven** and **modeled faith-walking** for Timothy.

Parents will be called and directed by God in different ways to pass on faith and trust in Him, depending on their setting and the unique needs of their children. Factored into this is also the emotional climate in the home. Each parent must seek God for creative and effective ways to pass on faith in God—which will serve as a **shield of protection** as their children grow and later as they become adults.

Without a shadow of a doubt, I know God called me to homeschool my children. In the middle of a transition from youth ministry in our district, the Gulf Latin American District, to taking a pastorate in **Crystal City, Texas**, I felt from the Lord that I should homeschool my children. As I read the Bible and sought the Lord, I became more intentional about learning what that would entail. I thought it would be difficult, yet if God was calling me to do this, I needed to obey and prepare.

I read, I studied, and I sought out curriculum that could meet their needs. In the fall of **1985**, when our daughter was entering third grade, I prayed that God would help me obey and do for Him what He knew was best for my children. This may not be what every parent is led to do—**each parent must seek God** on how to pass on the shield of faith to their children.

I was close to receiving my bachelor's degree in Christian Education, so I purposed that—along with homeschooling our daughter, caring for our 16-month-old son, and helping my husband in our new pastorate—I would slowly move toward earning my **Bachelor of Arts degree** to better serve my children. It was not easy—just a few college classes at a time—but by **1987** I earned my degree and continued homeschooling. With my husband's help, I homeschooled for **eight years**.

We saw how our obedience to do this during that specific time in our children's lives produced **servants of God** who fear the Lord, love Him, and who excelled academically when they transitioned to public school for their high school years.

Both went on to earn their Bachelor's degrees—**one in Education and the other in Pastoral Ministry** from Southwestern Assemblies of God University (now **Nelson University**). They are **blooming where they are planted**, doing ministry in a way that is different from how my husband and I do ministry—and they are touching lives we could never reach. May God continue to be glorified in their lives.

Parents, **do whatever God leads you to do** to better serve the needs of your children—but above all, **PASS IT ON—The Shield of Faith.** God knows them by name and knows what they need. He will lead you as you provide a loving atmosphere that fosters a fear of God, a love for learning, and that produces **servants for the Most High**.

It won't be like what another family does, but **you be prayerful** and do what **God leads you** to do.

Paul with Timothy and others, Elijah with Elisha, and Eunice and Lois (Loida) for Timothy all modeled God's plan. They poured themselves into the generations that followed to perpetuate faith in a living and powerful God.

There is a great urgency that the present generation contemplate the following question:

How can this generation ensure faith in God will be passed on to future generations?

The Bible gives guidance and help, as do others who have been confronted with this urgent need in the midst of a generation overwhelmed by social media and countless distractions.

The Bible personalities mentioned serve as great examples of how to pass faith to the next and subsequent generations. They mentored the next generation by letting them walk with them through the good, the happy, the productive, the sad, the lonely, the dangerous, and the difficult. They modeled for the next generation what "waiting on the Lord" and "obedience to the Lord" look like.

Paul and Elijah provided many opportunities for the next generation to see how God brings one through victoriously. Then, Lois (Loida) and Eunice, by teaching the Holy Scriptures and modeling faith in the all-powerful, all-loving, faithful God, impressed upon generations beyond theirs the importance of the **family and home in the passing on of faith**.

I would like to share one of the saddest, yet most impactful moments in my life—where faith was needed, and faith rose to meet the challenge.

I had been handed down, had learned about, and had always desired to have and pass on faith. And in this experience, **faith had its time to shine through**.

My daughter called me one afternoon with panic in her voice:

"Mom, something has happened to Kiara."

I heard her broken voice and could sense she was crying. That's all I needed to hear to take off and begin praying—with understanding and in the Spirit. I didn't know what to expect, I only knew it was serious and only God could intervene. The panic in my daughter's voice was enough to convey the seriousness of the moment.

I arrived at her home only to find both parents in tears, with the father holding a **lifeless child** in his arms, showing me—with tears in his eyes—that she was not breathing.

Something came over me—the Spirit of the Lord.

Later, as I reflected, I was reminded of the Scriptures that say,

"The Spirit of the Lord came upon him," when speaking of Samson tearing apart the lion with his bare hands (Judges 14:6), and again in 1 Samuel 16:13, when the Spirit of the Lord came upon David.

I felt that same Spirit come upon me. Though I saw a lifeless child in my son-in-law's arms, a voice from within me spoke clearly:

"Speak life into the child."

As I was about to speak life into my granddaughter, my son-in-law was weeping. I turned to him and said,

"Carlos, we are going to speak life into Kiara."

She lay limp, without signs of life, in his arms.

But then I felt God speak firmly to my heart:

"Not you. He, the father, must speak life into his child."

There was no doubt God was teaching both of us to obey. So I told him,

"Carlos, speak life into your child in the name of Jesus."

A little hesitant, but desperate to see life return, he quietly but firmly said,

"I speak life in the name of Jesus."

Immediately after he spoke those words, Kiara began to breathe and move her arms. They had already called EMS, and the team arrived soon after—but by the time they got there, God had already answered our prayer and honored the words my son-in-law declared **in the name of Jesus**.

Nothing is impossible for God.

And **without faith**, it is impossible to please God or see **miracles, signs, and wonders**.

That moment was an amazing experience for both of us—**a teachable moment** that God orchestrated to pass on the **shield of faith**.

No matter where life takes him, my son-in-law will never forget that experience. May it remain a memory that reminds him of: the power of God, the results of faith, and the authority he carries when he **speaks in obedience in the name of Jesus**.

I will never forget that day, and I pray my son-in-law never will either.

Beyond a shadow of doubt, God did a miracle—He brought our granddaughter **back to life**.

Kiara was about 2 or 3 years old then. Today, she is **21 years old**. She loves Jesus. She plays the **guitar, keyboard, and drums**. She lives for Him and shares His love in many ways. We've shared this story with her. She knows she is here because **God answered a prayer of faith**—and she knows He has a special purpose and plan for her life.

I would also like to share two more experiences—**stories that have been repeated often to our children**—that remind us of God's power and serve as wonderful **faith-passing moments**.

I still remember so vividly a faith-passing opportunity in **Albuquerque, New Mexico**. During one of our visits to see my mom and brothers, our son Eli—then about 8 years old—came running frantically to tell me what he had just discovered.

His tongue was hurting, and when he looked in the mirror, he saw it **full of blisters**. This startled him, and he came running with **tears in his eyes**, saying:

"Mom, look at my tongue!"

I could see the distress on his face and the white blisters covering his tongue.

I drew him close and hugged him. I said,

"Eli, we can pray—nothing is impossible for God."

We joined hands, and I said a simple prayer:

"Lord, nothing is impossible for You.

You know what Eli is going through and any pain he may be experiencing.

We ask You, in the name of Jesus, to bring healing to his tongue from those blisters.

Thank You, Lord, for hearing our prayer."

Immediately after our prayer, he headed for the restroom mirror. **His faith led him to believe God would work.** He looked in the mirror and found that all the blisters were gone. His tongue was completely normal. He came running to the kitchen—where we had prayed—leaping and with great excitement exclaimed,

"Mom, all the blisters are gone! God healed me! Thank you, Lord!"

Another faith-passing opportunity I experienced was when my daughter was about seven or eight years old. Her permanent teeth were beginning to grow in as her baby teeth became loose and were pulled out. We noticed immediately that the first few teeth were growing in crooked, but we thought they might straighten out as the other teeth began to grow in and take their place.

After about a year, it was evident that several of them had grown in very crooked.

She expressed concern about this periodically. On one occasion when she mentioned it, I told her we could pray and ask God to begin a work to straighten her teeth. At first, she just gave me a glance, as if to say, *"Yeah, right."* However, she agreed to join hands with me as we asked God, **in Jesus' name**, to straighten her teeth.

We prayed a **simple prayer**.

I told her I would continue praying and believing God to answer.

Approximately four months later, I began to see a difference in the formation of her teeth. I didn't say anything at first, but one month later, it was **evident something miraculous had happened**—those teeth were straightening up.

At that time, I brought it to her attention so she could observe what was taking place.

God was at work!

There was no denying that God was doing a work in her teeth. Before the year was over, all her teeth were straight, and any new ones that came in grew in beautifully. She will never forget what God did. **Her beautiful smile** reminds me of God's great power to perform miracles in answer to prayers offered up in faith.

Moments like these open opportunities to pass the shield of faith to our children and to the generations that come behind us.

Let's take advantage of those open doors to teach our children what faith in our living God can do. I thank God for that opportunity He granted me. My daughter is reminded daily, as she smiles, of the miracle God did.

I tell her,

"Dina, God gave you that beautiful smile to bless and uplift others. Don't hold back that smile—share it!"

My son will never forget what he experienced in answer to a prayer of faith.

My daughter, with that daily reminder of what God did for her, shares that experience with her family and others.

The shield of faith is passed on.

When doubts arise about God's power as they move forward in life and ministry, they can raise up the shield of faith they've taken up. It will extinguish the fiery darts aimed at their minds—to confuse them or make them doubt.

Faith is the expectation of miracles—expecting what we cannot see now, but holding on to the hope that it is coming.

Faith is the conviction, the certainty that **God can do anything**. It is knowing we can trust God—**His power, His timing**.

Faith in our lives leads us to a **complete surrender** to Him.

The Bible says **faith is our shield—our protection**.

I often use an illustration in sermons with my daughter. I hand her a shield and tell her it symbolizes the **faith I have passed on to**

her. It should be her protection against the devil's schemes and fiery darts.

I attempt to bombard her mind—she puts her shield up to protect her head, symbolizing how the fiery darts are aimed at our **minds and thoughts**. With her shield, she's able to protect her mind.

Then I go for her **heart**, because the devil shoots fiery darts at our children's hearts to cause distress, anguish, and brokenness. He wants them to give their hearts away to people or practices that interrupt their loving relationship with God. But again, she puts up her shield.

I shoot for her **feet**, so she cannot go share the gospel, for the Bible says: "How beautiful are the feet of those who bring good tidings of good things." (Romans 10:15) She puts up the shield to protect her feet.

Let's **Pass On the Shield of Faith**.

It is their **protection** against the fiery darts of the enemy.

What do you think the author of Hebrews means by writing that "faith is the assurance of things hoped for, the conviction of things not seen" (Heb 11:10)?

_____

_____

_____

_____

Is there a difference between faith and self-confidence? What do you think? _____ If yes, what is the difference?

_____

_____

_____

_____

Is there a difference between faith and positive thinking? What do you think? If yes, what is the difference?

_____

_____

_____

_____

Name two persons whom you have witnessed living by faith. What did you witness in their lives?

_____

_____

_____

_____

As you have read about faith, what is your honest desire to accomplish by faith?

_____

_____

_____

_____

Will you pursue the goal of passing on the SHIELD of faith?

_____

_____

_____

_____

Four Generations: Abedulia Padilla, (Great Grandma Lula)
Doris Loida Padilla Espinoza (Grandma Loida), Eunice
Espinoza Roiz with her daughter, Isela Roiz (Grandma Lula`s
Great Granddaughter}

Great Grandma Lula with her Great Granddaughter, Isela Roiz

PASSING ON THE FAITH

Like Lois (Loida) and Eunice, my mom was faithful to Pass on the Shield of Faith. I have strived to ensure my daugther has taken up the shield of faith. My daughter is passing on to her children the Shield of Faith. The Bible pictured here is falling apart due to being open and used so much throughout my mom's life. There is a poplular saying: "A person whose Bible is falling apart usually belongs to someone who isn't."

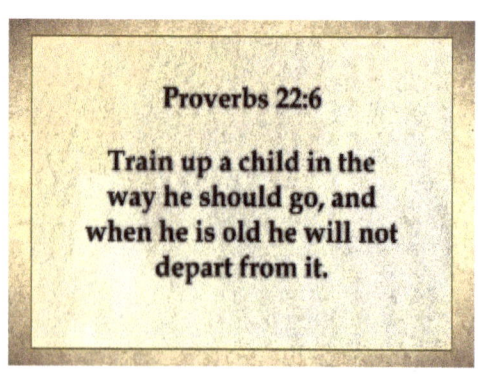

Proverbs 22:6

Train up a child in the way he should go, and when he is old he will not depart from it.

PASS IT ON

The

TORCH

OF

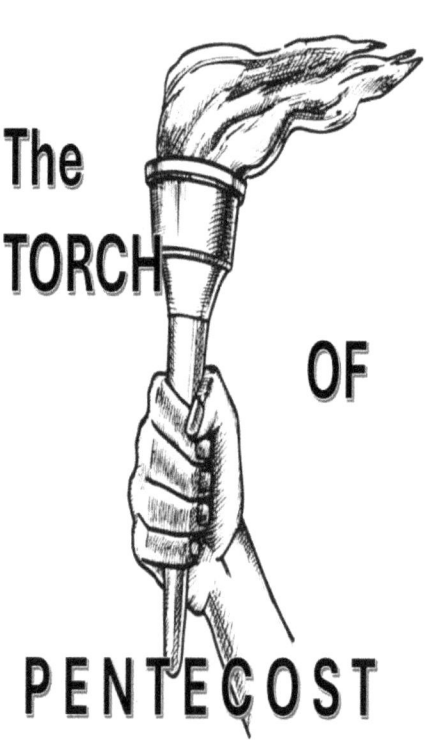

PENTECOST

Chapter 5

Pass It On-The Torch of Pentecost

As we have read in former chapters, the New Testament has many examples of servants of God who ensured that future generations would know and experience faith in God and the power that was promised to all believers. One such example is that of **Peter**, who—before the day of Pentecost—was denying that he even knew Jesus. Yet, when he was **filled with the Holy Spirit**, he became a powerful, dynamic vessel in the hands of the Lord.

In chapter 3 of John's Gospel, the **baptism of Jesus in the Jordan River** by John the Baptist appears. Prior to the Scripture describing Jesus' baptism, John declares:

"I indeed baptize you with water unto repentance, but he that cometh after me is mightier than I, whose shoes I am not worthy to

bear: he shall baptize you with the Holy Ghost, and with fire."
(John 3:11, KJV)

When Jesus ascends into heaven, He tells the disciples **not to leave Jerusalem**, but to go and wait for the promise. According to Acts 2, when the day of Pentecost had fully come, suddenly there came a sound **as of a rushing mighty wind**, and there appeared to them **cloven tongues like as of fire**, and it sat upon each of them. They were all **filled with the Holy Ghost** and began to speak in other tongues as the Spirit gave them utterance.

This created questions and confusion, because many people present heard them speaking in their own languages, and some assumed they were drunk.

Peter, filled with the Holy Spirit and fire, stood in the midst of the crowd and preached a dynamic message of repentance. He declared that **this promise is for them, for their children, and for their children's children**. The Bible says they gladly received his word, were baptized, and that **about three thousand souls** were added to them that day.

The powerful **torch of Pentecost** was ignited in those new believers' lives!

The entire book of Acts reflects Peter **sharing the power of the Holy Ghost** with believers, thus ensuring that **his and future generations** would experience the Holy Ghost and fire. In his anointed message, he repeats the promise made in the book of Joel:

"And it shall come to pass in the last days, saith God, I will pour out of my Spirit upon all flesh: and your sons and your daughters shall prophesy, and your young men shall see visions, and your old men shall dream dreams:

And on my servants and on my handmaidens I will pour out in those days of my Spirit; and they shall prophesy."

(Acts 2:17–18, KJV)

By the power of the Holy Spirit, Peter delivers a lasting reminder to all that as present and future generations **walk in this prophecy**, they will be empowered to witness and to experience the manifestation of **God's glory**.

I was blessed to have grandparents, **Rev. Tomás and Lugardita Martínez**, who—like Peter—were passionate that future generations be handed the **torch of Pentecost**. They instilled in us, through **devotionals, songs, choruses, sermons, and everyday living**, a hunger and a desire to be filled with the Holy Spirit—to walk in and live by the Spirit.

We were reminded of this truth daily—during chores, at mealtimes, and before bed.

They, along with my mom (whom everyone lovingly called **Lula**), would share with us how in the **late 1930s and early 1940s**, revival came to the areas of **Cuba, La Jara, and Gallina, New Mexico**. The move of God was so powerful that they would drive hours in **horse-drawn carts** for miles to witness what was happening—and with a hunger for what they had heard, they believed it would happen to them as well; and it did.

They were filled with the Holy Spirit and spoke in other tongues.

The revival services would end very late, and they would then travel back to their homes—about two hours away by cart or wagon. My mom shared on many occasions how, in the pitch-black night, **miraculously, a great light like a ball of fire** would appear above their wagons and lead them through the darkness until they arrived home.

I loved to hear her stories—how they would **sing all the way home** and how the **power of God** would fall upon them as they sang and prayed during their journey. Some would describe what they were feeling and experiencing.

Many nights, I would ask her to tell me the story again and again.

It interested me so much that I wanted to hear it every night.

Hearing these stories of their experiences **whetted in me an appetite for the divine—for the miraculous—for the power of God.**

Parents, share your personal stories with your children and grandchildren—especially your experiences with the Lord and the miracles you've witnessed. I wanted to know more every time my parents and grandparents would share how God was healing, saving, and baptizing in the Holy Spirit.

No doubt, your children and grandchildren will want to hear your stories, too.

They wholeheartedly embraced the truths written in the book of Acts—that **we would receive power when the Holy Spirit comes upon us.** We saw the power of God operating in their lives and ministries. We experienced and witnessed **miraculous healings** and **supernatural moves of God.** We heard them **pray in the Spirit** and with understanding. Their home was filled with the presence of God.

The **peace we felt** the moment we walked into their home is unforgettable.

I grew up as a child and young person with a longing to be filled with the Holy Spirit and to walk in that life of strength, power, healings, and miracles, as I saw my parents and grandparents live out before our eyes. We were taught to **desire** and **receive the baptism of the Holy Spirit**, with the initial evidence of speaking in tongues. They would teach us to **earnestly ask for** and be ready to receive the baptism of the Holy Spirit. So, I did.

Though many years went by and I did not receive that gift of speaking in tongues, they taught me to **keep believing** and to be ready to receive it. They taught me that **God has special timing**, and in His time, He would fulfill His promise to me.

I remember my mom, dad, and grandparents praying and speaking in tongues. At first, I was a bit scared, since I didn't understand what they were saying or what was happening. But as I asked and as they shared and explained more to me—using God's Word—I no longer feared. Instead, I felt a special presence of the Lord fill the room as they would pray in tongues. I wondered if that would ever happen to me. Would I ever speak in tongues, or was it just for grownups? They assured me that it was **for their children and grandchildren**, no matter the age.

I reached my teenage years and still had not had the experience I longed for. I just kept loving, serving, and moving forward with faith in my heart, believing that at the right time, **God would fulfill this promise in my life**. At a time in my youth when I was making choices and major decisions for my future, I experienced what I had so longed for.

At that point in my life, I was in a relationship with a very well-mannered and respectful young man, with whom I was becoming very serious. I was contemplating the possibility of a future with him. He was very religious and God-fearing. He had great goals and a bright future.

As I would pray and seek guidance concerning this relationship, something in my spirit would feel uneasy. I began to battle within myself: "How could this not be the right one for me? I love and care for him so much." I would ask God, "Why am I feeling such conflicting emotions? Why is this troubling me?"

The inner turmoil became so intense that it began to affect my studies and my daily life. When I could no longer bear the battle within, I told the Lord, "Lord, I can no longer deal with this turmoil, and I feel like you are asking me to end this relationship. Honestly, Lord, I cannot do this—but if You can, I give You permission to do it. It will hurt deeply, and I cannot do it—but it's in Your hands."

Meanwhile, we had gone out of town to attend a rally—which we could not get into because it was so full. In Spanish, we call these gatherings **"confraternidades."** Since we couldn't go in or hear the service, some young people (cousins and friends) decided we might as well drive to a nearby town for ice cream and then return in time for the service to end.

Something within me felt uneasy and fearful about leaving, but I went anyway. I really felt I needed to be in that service. Even though I was reluctant, I left with them.

However, the whole time we were gone, I felt anxious and nervous.

When we got back, they were saying the closing prayer, and everyone began greeting each other and saying their goodbyes. I felt a deep **impulse** within me to pray. I had felt bad about leaving, and I still had that longing to be in the service. I could not hide the burning desire I had to **run to the altar** and pray.

I didn't understand it, but it was so intense that I walked up to the pastor and asked him if he would mind if I knelt to pray while others were greeting one another. He said, "Sure." The pastor at that time was **Pastor Epimenio Abeyta**. He didn't hesitate to give me permission.

I threw myself to my knees and began to pray—and before I knew it, I was **speaking in tongues, fluently**, and feeling a power, anointing, and fire come over me. God had something in store for me that night, and I didn't even know it.

I cannot fully explain the combination of emotions I experienced that night—**joy, peace, contentment, power**, and a deep **sense of purpose** that this night would be a turning point in my life.

Indeed, everything in my life began to change from that moment on.

I had no idea how God would continue—through His Holy Spirit—to lead, guide, and open doors of opportunity. To this day, I stand amazed at how God works uniquely, **His wonders to perform**, fulfilling His divine purposes.

A burning desire to do God's will and a passion for souls like I had never experienced before began to fill my life. It became more intense daily as I began to **exercise the gift of praying in tongues**.

To parents and grandparents: I remind you to pray that your children and grandchildren **be saved and filled with the power of the Holy Spirit**. I know my parents and grandparents were praying for me. What I experienced was an **answer to prayer** and a **fulfillment of God's promise** in the Scriptures.

The **baptism of the Holy Spirit** and living in the Spirit will **revolutionize their lives**, transform them by the renewing of their minds, produce in them a new perspective for setting godly goals, and give them a deep desire to do what God wants them to do, to go where He wants them to go, and to be what He wants them to be.

I am a witness that this experience **transformed my heart**, brought **clarity to my mind**, and **directed me** in the paths God had planned for me. I want this for my children and grandchildren—and I know you do too.

I sincerely pray that **God will interrupt their lives and plans** like He did mine and show them His way and His will. I wonder now where I would be had I not heeded the **intense impulse** to go pray at the altar of that little church—**Templo Cristiano in El Rancho, New Mexico.**

At that time, I was in the middle of college, pursuing plans to become a computer programmer and later a systems analyst. At the young age of 18, I was already on a **work-study program** in data processing that was paying me **very high wages** for my age.

I—and my professors—had big plans. Upon graduating from this program, I was expected to land a high-paying job. I thought I was on top of the world and headed for success.

But in the middle of all that—**suddenly**, I was baptized in the Holy Spirit. My life spun around, and God began tenderizing my heart more and more. Ultimately, I felt a **call to more of God** and more service to Him and for Him.

I began to understand that this could be what some call "**a call to ministry**." I wasn't sure, but I began processing this in my heart and spirit. I prayed, "Lord, how will I know?"

Soon after, I attended a service at my home church, **Aposento Alto Assembly of God in Albuquerque, New Mexico**, where a guest speaker from Durango City, Durango, Mexico—**Rev. Antonio Rivera**—was preaching that night. He was, at that time, the director of the Bible School in that city.

At the end of his message, there was a **message in tongues**, followed by an **interpretation**, which he delivered. From what I remember, the words he spoke went something like this:

"Do not doubt Me any longer, My child. It is I who have called you. You don't have to question that any longer. If you will heed to My call and obey My voice, I will guide you every step of the way. You will experience My power and go to places that right now, you cannot even imagine. Say, 'Yes' to My will and My way."

I **ran to the altar** that night, knelt, and said, "Yes, Lord, to Your will and to Your way." That night, **my calling to ministry was confirmed**.

Later, I heard a song by that very title—*"Yes, Lord, Yes"*—and I could relate so deeply to the message it conveys.

<u>Yes, Lord, Yes – by Shirley Ceasar</u>

I'll say yes, Lord, yes

To your will and to your way

I'll say yes, Lord, yes

I will trust you and obey

When your Spirit speaks to me

With my whole heart I'll agree

And my answer will be yes, Lord, yes

Verse:

Lord, I give you all the glory

For all You've given me

You have filled my life until I overflow

I'm yours to use

In an anyway You choose

You are Lord of all, so how can I say no?

verse 2

If I never knew the fullness

of living in your will

I would never know how rich my life would be

Lord, my willingness to serve is the least that you deserve.

To this day, my husband and I continue to sing that song. We press on in our mid-70s with a daily surrender to His will and to His way—**loving this journey in Him**.

Perhaps the enemy sensed something was in the making and tried to put detours in the road to keep me from attending that service in *El Rancho* the night of the rally (*confraternidad*). But I truly believe that, in answer to the prayers of my parents and grandparents, God placed in me a **hunger for Him** and a **passionate desire to receive the baptism of the Holy Spirit**.

That longing I had—to receive the **Torch of Pentecost**— overcame any obstacle that Satan tried to place in my path.

When I most needed power, comfort, and boldness to face the breaking of a relationship, **God filled me with the Holy Spirit and fire**. When I was facing one of the most complex decisions of my life, the precious promise of the Holy Spirit came like a mighty river to flood my soul. It felt like a **torch that burned within me**.

I rose from that experience full of joy and peace that overcame the turmoil I had been experiencing in my heart.

That same week, it wasn't me—but my boyfriend—who came to break off the relationship. I didn't know what was going on in his heart or mind, but he simply said he had to do this.

It **hurt deeply**, and I cried. We had dated for about 2½ years. But even in that heartbreak, there was an **undeniable peace** in my spirit—a peace that passes all understanding.

We both cried. He said he didn't understand why he was doing this, but he just felt he needed to. His final words stirred my spirit:

"I just feel like you are in God's hands, and who am I to take you out of God's hands?"

That line stayed with me:

In God's hands is where I always want to be.

The Holy Spirit was my constant companion in that difficult time—filling me with comfort and giving me hope to face the future without someone I had loved and dreamed with.

Maybe as you read this, **God is prompting your heart** about a relationship that needs to be turned over to Him so He can fulfill His perfect will. If so, please be obedient. Surrender it to Him— **He'll do the rest**. I have **never regretted** the breakup that transpired. You won't either when you acknowledge the truth of His Word:

"For my thoughts are not your thoughts, neither are your ways my ways," declares the Lord.

"As the heavens are higher than the earth, so are my ways higher than your ways and my thoughts than your thoughts."

(Isaiah 55:8–9, NIV)

You see, I had been walking, living, and planning **my ways**—not **His ways**. But God's call had been on my life **from the time I was in my mother's womb**.

My mother once shared with me that when she was expecting me, her doctor advised her to **consider terminating the pregnancy** due to complications with her health. Since she already had five children, the doctor said having another baby could put her life at risk. He reminded her that those five children needed their mother.

I've pondered that many times—how **God's call was always there**. Yet, for a season, I wasn't tuned into His voice. I was like a radio stuck on the wrong frequency—just noise and static. But when the **Holy Spirit cleared the interference**, I finally heard **the clear sound of God's voice**, drawing me to Himself. That's when **God's plans and purposes began to be transmitted** into my life.

My brother José once shared a powerful story that relates so well to this idea. He was a Morse code intercept operator, trained to pick up and analyze enemy Russian transmissions. He had to **calibrate his receiver** to distinguish friendly signals from enemy ones—to isolate and decipher the right message among the noise.

It struck me—**that's exactly what the Holy Spirit does for us.** He helps us calibrate our hearts and minds to discern God's voice amid the distractions and spiritual noise of this world. Without that spiritual calibration, we risk missing God's guidance.

The **Holy Spirit continues to be my daily companion**, preparing me for whatever each day will bring. I am eternally grateful for those who went before me—those who were faithful to **pass on the Torch of Pentecost.**

Shortly after receiving the baptism of the Holy Spirit, **God called me to ministry**, and I responded. I left my hometown and family to pursue His call, confident that God had made a way for me to follow His purpose. I enrolled in Latin American Bible Institute in El Paso, Texas to study God's word and prepare for ministry.

Now, I continue to proclaim to the generations that follow the **power and truth of God**. Like Peter, I want to be sure to **pass on the Torch of Pentecost**.

May those who come after me also be led to **hear and to heed to His will and His way**, just as I did. I cannot live without the **daily guidance of the Holy Spirit**. I cannot make it without **His discernment and illumination**.

The Holy Spirit is God. One symbol of the Holy Spirit is **fire**, because He purifies and illuminates. Jeremiah described the Word of God, the move of God, and the power of the Holy Spirit in his life as "like a fire that burns within—a fire shut up in my bones" (Jeremiah 20:9).

God may, at times, give us a message to deliver that is difficult to speak—just as He did with Jeremiah. Jeremiah would grow frustrated with the struggle of what God asked him to say. Not wanting to continually deliver words of gloom or judgment, he sometimes chose to remain silent. But that only increased his inner turmoil.

Scripture suggests there were times he wanted to abandon his prophetic ministry because of the rejection and ridicule he faced. Yet the fire within—that torch in his spirit—rose to the surface, and he could not remain silent. The Bible expresses this in **Jeremiah 20:9 (NET)**:

"Sometimes I think, 'I will make no mention of his message. I will not speak as his messenger anymore.' But then his message becomes like a fire locked up inside of me, burning in my heart and soul. I grow weary of trying to hold it in; I cannot contain it."

So strong was the power of God within him that it overrode any feelings of discouragement and dread. He was **constrained to speak**. I love how the Wycliffe Bible (WYC) expresses it:

"But the word of the Lord was made to me like a fire swelling in my heart, and enclosed in my bones; and I failed, and could not bear it, and so I had to speak it out."

Other translations add depth:

"I could not hold back." (KJV)

"I am weary of holding it in, and I cannot endure it." (NASB)

"I'm tired of holding it. In fact, I can't." (NIRV)

"And I am weary with holding it back, and I could not." (OJB, RGT)

I can relate to what Jeremiah expresses—a fire within. I **must** talk about the Word of God. It is **good news of great joy and salvation** for all the world. Though some may reject or ridicule those who proclaim the Word, we must, like Jeremiah, **speak it forth**.

The power of the Holy Spirit **moves me to proclaim the truth** about God's love and the power of Pentecost. I cannot keep silent.

The Holy Spirit is the One who **comforts, guides, illuminates, inspires, and anoints** me to serve God and carry out His call on my life. He is the One who drew me in from the life I was living and opened my understanding to God's love and purpose for me. I want others to experience what was opened up to me.

How sad to think someone could be lost for eternity because **I kept silent**. I thank God for the pastors and evangelists who did not remain silent as I was growing up.

The truth of Pentecost that we must pass on is the knowledge of the **work of the blessed Holy Spirit**, who brings conviction and lights up the darkness with the light of God's truth, ways, and purposes. The **Torch of Pentecost** is the experience of being **baptized in the Holy Spirit**, with the evidence of speaking in tongues—a language of prayer and mystery that the enemy cannot understand but certainly feels the impact of.

The enemy is **weakened** in his hold on areas and individuals when God's people **exercise this gift** that empowers their Christian walk.

Will you be faithful to **pass on the Torch of Pentecost**?

Your answer can only be "yes" if that torch is **burning within you**. If you feel you are missing that fire and power, even now as you read this, **ask God to fill you with the Holy Spirit and fire**.

Once you experience His power, assurance, peace, comfort, and guidance—by being immersed in the river of His Spirit—you will **never be the same**. You, too, will want to pass on the **Torch of Pentecost** to those who come behind you.

The Holy Spirit is **real**, and the promise of the baptism is fulfilled as we stay **close to the Giver**, Jesus. He is, according to

John the Baptist, **the One who baptizes with the Holy Spirit and with fire**.

That fire **continues to burn within me**. That Torch of Pentecost burns so deeply that I want to take advantage of every opportunity to **PASS IT ON** to all who will listen—or to anyone willing to walk with me and **experience the difference** in daily life when that **Torch of Pentecost** burns within.

The Bible says in **Acts 1:8**:

"And you shall receive power when the Holy Spirit comes on you, and you shall be my witnesses in Jerusalem, and in all Judea and Samaria, and to the uttermost parts of the earth." (NIV)

If anyone reading this **earnestly desires** the baptism of the Holy Spirit, **do not give up**. Jesus is with you, and **you are safe in His hands**. As we seek **the Giver, not just the gift**, He fulfills His promises in His time.

Yield to His purposes. Trust His timing. **Rest** in the safety of His hands as you wait for the promise.

Desiring this experience, asking for it, knowing it is a **gift**— this is what God is looking for. You do not need to feel pressure or despair if it doesn't happen immediately. Just keep believing, desiring, and asking. **Live close to the Master, Jesus.**

Luke 11:13 reads as follows (AMP):

"If you, then, being evil [that is, sinful by nature], know how to give good gifts to your children, how much more will your heavenly Father give the Holy Spirit to those who ask and continue to ask Him."

I asked—and kept on asking. When I began to feel anxious, wondering why others were being baptized in the Holy Spirit and speaking in other tongues while I had not yet received this experience, God—along with my parents and grandparents—helped me understand something very important: what God desired from me was not frustration, but **relationship**. He wanted me to **draw close to Jesus daily**—to live safe in His arms through **reading His Word, prayer**, and **holy living**.

What I needed to do was **dedicate myself to Him fully**, while continuing to ask for the fulfillment of His promise. And just at the **right time—God's time**—I was baptized in the Holy Spirit.

So I encourage you: **keep asking, keep believing, keep drawing close to the Lord**. It is in that closeness and intimacy with Him that, **when you least expect it**, the Holy Spirit can fill your life with power from on high.

Yes, Paul mentored Timothy and passed on to him a **baton of service**. Timothy took that baton and ran with it. Scripture records the many ways Timothy served, clearly inspired by Paul's example. Elijah led Elisha and walked faithfully with the all-powerful God, and as a result, **Elisha received the mantle of God's anointing** and walked in double the prophetic power.

The **faith that lived in Timothy's grandmother, Lois, and his mother, Eunice,** was passed on to him through daily doses of prayer, scripture, and godly instruction. That firm foundation prepared Timothy to become the Apostle Paul's close companion and co-laborer, ultimately continuing the work of the early church after Paul's departure to heaven.

Peter, too, was **transformed by the Holy Spirit** into a bold, dynamic vessel who proclaimed the Word of God with clarity and power. Through him, thousands were added to the church, and the **torch of Pentecostal fire** spread through villages and cities. Peter's ministry, empowered by the Holy Spirit, left behind a clear **legacy of surrender and supernatural living**.

How we need **parents, grandparents, uncles, aunts, neighbors, educators, and friends** in our communities today to be these kinds of role models to our **children, youth, and young adults**. Oh, that this generation would not just hear about faith or read about the Spirit-filled life, but **see it modeled before their eyes**—people walking in the Spirit, living by the Spirit, praying in the Spirit, and **burning with Holy Ghost fire**.

What a difference it would make if faith were seen and not only spoken—**lived out, not just taught**.

Those **District Youth Directors** passed on the **Torch of Pentecost** as they **preached about the Holy Spirit and power**, and intentionally **led youth into life-changing encounters** with the fire from heaven. As a result, we now see many of the youth who were mentored under their leadership **ministering in pastorates and other ministries with power and boldness**.

Dino Espinoza, Moses Cavazos. JR Rodriguez and Charlie Rivera are actually holding torches, provided by Mike Fernandez and his staff as they related the importance of "Passing the Torch of Pentecost." A big thanks to Mike for this visual illustration to the youth of the Gulf Latin American District. Those present will never forget your illustration of such powerful truths.

Let's all be intentional about **Passing the Torch of Pentecost. May the teaching of the book of Acts, and the example of Peter's ministry in the power of the Holy Spirit and passing of the torch of Pentecost serve as a model we all imitate.**

We have been challenged to Pass the Baton of Service, to Pass the Mantle of Anointing, to Pass the Shield of Faith, and lastly to Pass on the Torch of Pentecost.

My Grandparents, Lugardita Sandoval Martinez and Rev. Tomás Martinez passed on the Torch of Pentecost to our family.

My parents, Abedulia Martinez Padilla and José Leandro Padilla were faithful to Pass on the Torch of Pentecost.

II Timothy 1:14: That good thing which was committed to you, keep by the Holy Spirit who dwells in us.

A torch needs fuel and purpose. What will keep you lit with Pentecost?

_____

_____

_____

_____

How can you use the presence of the Holy Spirit in your life and in the life of others to strengthen the unity of the body of Christ?

_____

_____

_____

_____

Generational influence is a key to passing the torch. What have you seen others do that influence you to become a true disciple?

_____

_____

_____

_____

In what ways can you fan into flame the Holy Spirit who was given to you when you were forgiven and became part of the family of God?

_____

_____

_____

_____

Has anyone shared with you about the torch of Pentecost?

_____

_____

_____

_____

Have you been baptized in the Holy Spirit? _____ If so, have you noticed a difference in your life? _____Have others noticed the difference? _____. If not, would you like to be baptized in the Holy Spirit and speak in tongues? _____

It is a gift for all. God sees, hears, and listens. Elaborate on your desire in the form of a prayer:

_____

_____

_____

_____

_____

Jot down any questions you may have on the baptism in the Holy Spirit. The Word of God has answers and you can seek out a trusted pastor or minister who can help you find answers to your questions using the scriptures.

_____

_____

_____

_____

_____

Salvation comes through Jesus. We are saved by grace through faith and the Holy Spirit comes to dwell in us. Speaking in tongues as the initial evidence of baptism in the Holy Spirit empowers Christians for powerful witnessing and spiritual warfare.

How Can This Generation Ensure Faith in God Will Be Passed On to Future Generations?

**PASSING DOWN THE FAITH,
A BIBLICAL EXAMPLE**

Chapter 6

How Can This Generation Ensure Faith in God Will Be Passed On to Future Generations?

Youth and children of this present generation are so exposed to technology, with its conveniences and its quick responses, that it is hard to carry heart-to-heart and eye-to-eye conversations. The addiction that often develops with texting, emails, Facebook, Twitter, TikTok, Instagram, and Snapchat leaves children and youth distracted and continually checking for more instant communication. Adults are not exempt from distractions and looking for instant communication. We are so accessible to others and others to us. It is a sad sight to see a family eating a meal together in a restaurant, yet to see children and adults alike texting or engrossed in their hand-held devices. Texting is the new talking. According to *Good Housekeeping Magazine*, December 2009, the average teen sends and receives about 2,900 texts per month, almost 100 messages per day—more than six times the average in 2007. Then *Deseret News/Deseret Magazine* on September 27, 2023, according to a *Deseret News* study, said half of all teens get at least 237 texts per day.

Though there is no conclusive data, some psychologists express concern that over-texting may cause anxiety and sleep problems. To avoid this, the article "Too Much Texting?" by Laura Hahn shares a recommendation by Sherry Turkle, Ph.D., professor and director of the Initiative on Technology and Self at the Massachusetts Institute of Technology. She recommends that families seriously consider fighting back on texting by establishing text-free zones, like the dinner table and the car. Safeguarding mealtimes and drives to and from school activities can make those times special for communication with family.

Letting phones rest at night and requiring phones be charged somewhere other than in the bedroom will be extremely helpful to the entire family. According to Turkle, many kids are texting until 4 or 5 AM. Another recommendation is for parents to be role models. Being a role model for the children and youth is one of the most powerful ways to curtail so much texting. Textaholics say their parents are always on their mobiles. Unplug; your kid may follow suit.

The challenge before the Church of Jesus Christ, whether they be parents, teachers, pastors, friends, or relatives, is to have an entrance into teens' and children's worlds with all its distractions and pass on the faith. Technology continues to advance and provide new and more powerful devices that make access to youth and children so quick, providing location of individuals at every moment. What a danger!

Other distractions for youth are substance abuse, sex, and gangs. Church youth are lured into participating in these through peer pressure, and many succumb to the temptation. It is crucial that the present generation invest time and presence to be there for the young ones so trust and confidence can be built, making dialogue and relationship possible.

In an article by Phyllis Tickle entitled "My Six Essentials for Passing on the Faith," she writes the following statement:

"What we want to implant is easy and natural affection for the holy, an inherent connectedness to an ongoing story, and a sense of membership within a sustaining community that, being larger than any of us, is always there to hold all of us as well as demand some things of us."

In this article, the recommendation for teaching any long-lasting principle, truth, or faith in God is, first, to be honest with spouses and extended family, letting them know how serious one is about family youngsters being Christians and in what ways. It makes sense that if the family and extended family are aware of one's intentions, they can be of great help in ensuring that goal is met. Our parents, grandparents, and siblings were so supportive in helping my husband and me in helping us cement the Christian principles we upheld that were serious matters to us for our children.

The second recommendation is to earnestly pray for children, without them there, joining with the extended family for spiritual growth and progress for their souls. I say, "pray with them there and without them there." Prayer is powerful. Libraries are full of books that stand as living testimonies of wayward children who came to the Lord because of intercessory prayer. An old saying heard through the years is: "A family that prays together stays together." My parents modeled for us the priority of prayer for families to thrive. Anytime we were with them, they called us to prayer. We got to hear them pray and learned to pray as we heard them call out to God. Our parents prayed for us before we left for school. They prayed for us without us there and with us there, as well. They prayed every time we were beginning a trip. We did not partake of food at the table without saying a prayer of thanks. We witnessed them on their knees praying for us by name. Surely, I and many of you are blessed with parents and grandparents who modeled how important prayer is. However, if that was not your experience, you can begin it for your children, who will pass it on to their children. It's never too late to start that legacy of powerful godly influence.

The third recommendation, based on Judaism, recommends a special family prayer time in the evening. This has sometimes been called a "family altar," providing time for family thanksgiving and corporate worship. I grew up in the fifties when families of all faiths had evening devotions in their homes. We would be playing outside in the lovely weather of summer evenings, or bundled up and playing on winter evenings, when the call would come from our parents and the parents of our friends that it was time to come in for a devotional time together. As the decades have passed, this has become more uncommon.

The fourth is storytelling without the use of books or DVDs, though they have their benefit. I loved it when our parents or grandparents would share with us stories of how they met, how they were saved, or how they survived difficult times in their families. I was thrilled when they would share stories of their childhood or youth. I learned so much from them and cherish the memories of those special times. This provided for ad-libbing and for stories of faith to be spontaneous, depending on what was appropriate in everyday happenings of life for special teaching moments. So many times, their stories soothed my doubts and calmed my fears. Children have fears that can rob their sleep or bring inner turmoil and anxiety to their hearts and minds. It's these times of looking to God and His Word as a family that can help children overcome obstacles and fears they face each day with confidence as they become more aware of God's love and power. The Bible instructs believers:

"And ye shall teach them to your children, speaking of them when thou sittest in thine house, and when thou walkest by the way, when thou liest down, and when thou risest up." – Deut. 11:9 (KJV)

"Impress them on your children. Talk about them when you sit at home and when you walk along the road, when you lie down and when you get up." – Deut. 6:7 (KJV)

My only surviving aunt, Isabel Martinez Sanchez, tells of a time as a little girl in the 1930s when my grandpa was called to pray for a family whose family member was dying. The road was long, and by the time they got there, she had died. She says she remembers my grandpa and a member from church praying that God would bring her to life again. I am not sure if it was hours later, but she did come back to life, and my aunt remembers the lady asking, "Why did you bring me back? I was so peacefully resting in the arms of my Savior." This left an impact on my aunt. She recounted how it seemed years ago, faith to believe for healings and speaking life into lives of individuals who had already died was so much more prevalent. She witnessed this and many more miracles. May we be inspired to believe for more.

The fifth recommendation is music—passing on the beloved songs that instill and promote the faithfulness of God. Teaching those songs that exalt God's name, that proclaim His greatness, that have ministered in difficult times becomes the family's heritage. I vividly recall choruses and songs my grandparents or parents would sing after our devotions at night, which we called "the family altar." Even today, when I hear certain gospel songs, it takes me back to moments at our home altar time with my parents or grandparents. We had great moments together at those prayer times. Many of us were healed during those prayer times. Some of the songs we sing now, which we learned during those times, remind me of revivals, special services, or turnarounds in my life.

Our family is a musical family, so we sang our heartaches away, expressed our joy and celebration with and through music, and made it through difficult times through singing. Many of us wrote songs using God's Word as a guide to take us through some of the most difficult times in our lives. Pass on those powerful anthems, songs of worship, the tunes that have helped you overcome. Intentionally integrate them into your everyday living. Include them in difficult times you encounter. Your children will pass on those beloved melodies. I know our family has, and it has made a difference and changed our perspective on events of life. My family, the Padilla family, as a group and individually, have recorded many of the songs we have written, plus other songs we heard and liked—songs that touched our hearts and which we believed would touch others. When we are called home to be with Jesus, our voices and those songs will live on since they are on CDs and on YouTube. I love having access to my older brothers', the Padilla Brothers', recordings. I live far from my brothers, but when I hear their songs, I feel like I am close by them. Those songs bring me comfort, they encourage me, they make me happy, and when I am sad, I feel free to weep and pray as I listen to the touching messages those songs bring.

A sixth recommendation is food. The long-lasting impression and the delight to the palate that food associated with events leaves in the minds and taste buds of children is sure to be passed on if shared.

Our forebearers in the faith used to use that double reinforcement of food and event more or less unselfconsciously; but it is an art, a grace, and a legitimate ploy that we have somehow lost or misplaced along the way.

My taste buds come to life when I taste something that resembles the taste of my grandma's and my mom's cooking. Grandma seemed to season and cook meat in a way that made it so tasty, and though it seemed like so little, we always had enough for numerous cousins, aunts, uncles, and neighbors that dropped in. I never understood how, but now I recall how Grandma would pray, "Lord, multiply the little food we have—may it feed us all who are here;" —and it sure did—we were all fully satisfied and never left hungry.

I remember the biscuits and the chili my dad made. My mom was famous for her "Natillas," a New Mexican tasty dessert that resembles pudding with a meringue. I try to replicate this amazing dessert. In our golden years, my husband and I cook a lot. He has Dino's Diner and I have Loida's Kitchen. We work together to serve appetizing, colorfully plated, nutritious meals. Our children and grandchildren get to taste some of our dishes and will, no doubt, want to cook them when we are gone, and then they will pass them on to their children. With the succulent, tasty meals come eye-to-eye contact and heart-to-heart conversations that have left me longing to ensure our family has those special mealtimes where we talk about our faith, God's goodness, and provision daily. Don't skip mealtimes or abandon those times at the table together. Intentionally plan for the palate to be delighted and provide that time for meaningful conversations to take place.

The Bible's examples and the history of great persons who have had the widest influence in passing on faith and spreading Christianity were not those who taught with theory, but those who taught and led by example. God is counting on this generation to do our part in perpetuating the faith. It will not always be easy. There is a price to pay. It takes time, energy, and money to make passing of faith happen. It is not always convenient, but so productive.

The Bible characters paid a price, others have paid a price, and this generation will have to pay a price and intentionally invest time away from social media and electronic gadgets to ensure that faith is passed on. It will take intentionality to teach and prepare leaders. We can get comfortable in our present positions or with our titles and forget we have a generation behind us that needs to learn from us, and as they do, we will release the baton of service so they can continue our work and leap further and higher than we did. Quick and constant accessibility in our times can rob time needed to train, walk with our children, talk with our children, hear their questions, and sense their need. May God help us to lead by example.

Dr. Myles Munroe, before his death, spoke about a dream he had wherein he saw an athlete in a coffin with a baton in his hand. He says he understood what it was about. It was about people dying with a baton, and instead of passing it on, died with it. He went on to say that people would rather die (hold on to a position) than pass it on and live to see the others run on. This is not to say that persons who die while in a position or with a title have not passed on the baton, for many have passed on the baton the whole time they have been in a position. If they die, the work goes on because of what they taught and how they trained others to be ready should anything happen to them—sickness, life-changing events, or death. However, the dream depicts the danger of not preparing a successor and a lack of willingness to train, teach, and delegate to give others opportunities to learn and not willing to pass on the baton when it was obviously time to do so.

He mentioned how the young person, who is supposedly next, must go to the casket and pry the baton out of the dead man's hand just to take it to the next leg. He saw this as a struggle. He perceived this as a crucial dilemma in leadership. According to Dr. Munroe, effective leaders always prepare their replacements.

Paul, Elijah, Lois/Eunice, and Peter are biblical examples that modeled the passing on of service, of anointing, of faith, and Pentecostal power. May each generation be diligent to pass on the faith. Following intentional practices, this generation can ensure faith in God will be passed on to the future generations.

May the footprints of each generation lead the future generations to believe.

Let's walk with them, talk with them, lead them, teach them, help them be ready to be our successors.

Grandpa Dino with his grandsons, Jadon and Levi Espinoza, Mateo Roiz

PASSING ON THE SHIELD OF FAITH

Grandma Loida & Grandpa Dino with their daughter, Dina, and their granddaughters: Rosio,Kiara, Sofia, Isela, Briza and "Mateo, mi Timoteo." Ensuring our FAITH is passed on to future generations.

Grandma Loida with her daughter, Dina, and children. Great meals together. Great memories are brought to life when we remember times at the table.

Looking forward to the famous NATILLAS I made-a dessert I watched my mom make in this same pot. I believe they taste great because they are made in the origianl pot she used. Maybe my daughter and grandaughters will learn to make "Natillas", and I'll leave them that same pot---Yummy, Delicious!

Name some activities or customs that you are practicing of the recommendations given above or others you have determined for teaching any long-lasting principle, truth, or faith in God to those generations behind you, whether they are family members or not?

_____

_____

_____

_____

_____

_____

_____

What are some areas you would like to work on and things you can plan to make this happen?

_____

_____

_____

_____

_____

Have you ever experienced a family altar, a devotional time together as a family during the day or before you go to bed? _____ How often? _____ Will you try to carve time out of your day or before bed to try to bring the family together to read God's word and pray? It doesn't have to be long, but can you intentionally try to plan for that?_____

What are the titles to some songs your family likes and sings?

_____

_____

_____

_____

_____

What memories surface when you hear those songs?

_____

_____

_____

_____

_____

What are some recipes or foods you love that your family enjoys?

_____

_____

_____

_____

_____

Are you praying for your family members daily?_____If so, pray with them and for them. If you are not, determine today to pray for and with them daily.

THE PADILLA SIBLINGS

Top Row: Sylvia Fabiola
Next Row: Jose, Lee Roy, Paul Hugging Doris Loida, Eloy,

Top Row: Lee Roy, Paul, Clifford, Jose Leandro, Jr.

Doris Loida, Eloy, Sylvia Fabiola

Eloy, Paul/ Loida, Jose/Lee Roy, Sylvia

My mom & siblings after Dad died

To the glory of God and in answer to the prayers of faith of our parents and grandparents, we are all serving the Lord and are 74 – 82 years of age, and all 6 have celebrated their golden anniversaries and beyond.

IT'S

Chapter 7

It's Our Turn

Steve Green sings a song written by Jon Mohr that addresses the need for each of us to consider and ensure that those who come behind us find us faithful.

We cannot expect anyone to do or share what God has given each one of us individually to leave to those who come behind us. May the words of this song inspire, motivate, and challenge you to let the fire of your devotion light their way as they navigate their own journeys. It has spoken to my life and re-iterated what God has spoken to my heart time and time again.

Find Us Faithful by Jon Mohr - II Timothy 4:7-8

We're pilgrims on the journey of the narrow road

And those who've gone before us line the way

Cheering on the faithful, encouraging the weary

Their lives a stirring testament to God's sustaining grace

Surrounded by so great a cloud of witnesses

Let us run the race not only for the prize

But as those who've gone before us, let us leave to those behind us

The heritage of faithfulness passed on through godly lives.

Chorus

Oh, may all who come behind us find us faithful.

May the fire of our devotion light their way.

May the footprints that we leave, lead them to believe

And the lives we live inspire them to obey.

Oh, may all who come behind us find us faithful

After all our hopes and dreams have come and gone

And our children sift through all we've left behind

May the clues that they discover and the memories they uncover

Become the light that leads them to the road we each must find.

****

My mom was a woman of prayer who, in her lifetime, passed on to my siblings and me the baton of service, the mantle of anointing, the shield of faith, and the torch of the Holy Spirit. I am passionate about passing on to the next generation what God considers so essential and important for Kingdom and eternity purposes. As I watched my mom's life ebb away as a result of cancer, God's Holy Spirit enlightened me to see something amazing transpire right before my eyes. I would like to share my mom's last hours on this earth. I trust you understand the uniqueness of this transferring of one generation to the other.

When we are building, we hammer in nails to join wood, but to secure it, we bend the nail down to ensure the fastening or joining doesn't fall apart or separate. We call that *clenching*. God uses people and experiences to *clench* the faith that has been hammered in to join us to God.

By sharing some reflections of my mom's last hours, I trust it will be uplifting to all of us and *clench* in even stronger the faith she and others have handed down to us. In caring for Mom, I began my shift about 11:30 p.m. or 11:45 p.m. on March 29th, and after midnight she continued to breathe as she had been breathing the previous days, but her feet began to get cold. I stayed up most of the wee hours of the morning with her—loving her, singing to her, and praying. She would make facial expressions of pain or discomfort. Her last medication time was 3:20 a.m., and she was calm for a while, but I kept loving her and caressing her, praying for her, and worshipping God. About 3:45 a.m., I began to feel her hands get cold, and her sighs, which I had been hearing throughout those hours, became faint. I began speaking in tongues. The Bible says that the Spirit helps us in our weaknesses when we don't know what to pray for. The Bible describes it as praying in the Spirit. According to Romans 8:26:

"In the same way the Spirit comes to us and helps us in our weakness. We do not know what prayer to offer or how to offer it as we should, but the Spirit Himself knows our need and at the right time intercedes on our behalf with sighs and groanings too deep for words." (Amplified Bible)

An awesome presence of God began to fill the room in such a special way, especially at the head of her bed where I was praying and soothing her forehead—then suddenly I began to sing in English in a tone of voice not my own, and some beautiful words were coming from my mouth which I knew were not known words I had ever penned or sung. They were flowing so quickly and evenly in a melody so pretty that I wanted to grab my phone to record it as I have done when God has inspired me to write other songs. I could not move—the presence of God was so real and rich in that space where I was standing that I could not move to get my phone.

I understood in my spirit that God was letting me know that this song was not one for recording, nor one that we would ever hear again. It was a special song for Mom as she transitioned from this life to His eternal rest. It was His for her, for now. He assured me she was hearing this song on her flight to glory. I thought to myself, "I am singing the last song she will hear on earth, but she'll arrive in heaven and be serenaded by angels." Right after that, I felt her hands totally cold, her upper chest getting cold, her heartbeat almost gone, and her breath shallow and only coming out of her mouth. She was no longer breathing with her lungs. Only small breaths of air were coming from her mouth.

It was time for my sister Sylvia's shift. I called Sylvia and told her I thought we were losing Mom and that it would not be long, so I asked her to please call Anna, my niece, who was in another room in the house. I asked her to also call Eloy, who could call the Hospice staff.

Anna, my niece, got to see Mom give her last breath. Her face was still warm, but no more breath, no more heartbeat. I closed her eyes softly as they had a tiny slit or opening lately as she rested. She had made it! Her labor was over! I continued speaking to her, words like, "We love you, Mama! You're a CHAMP, Mama, you made it home! What are you seeing? God is faithful, you will rejoice for eternity."

I quoted a few Bible verses I had been quoting about heaven and her mansion – "Enjoy! Rejoice, Mama!" I declared. I had heard, and she had told me, that hearing is the last thing to go, so I have practiced, when at the bedside of anyone who passes, to keep speaking words of love, hope, and faith even after the last breath.

Mom had shared with me all the experiences she had when she accompanied her sisters and her parents to their last breath, and I had always prayed that God would give me the honor of being at her bedside in her last hours to pray and sing with her till her last breath was gone—as she had been faithful to do with her mom, her dad, her sisters, and others. I am forever grateful to God for giving me the desire of my heart. Psalm 37:4 says, "Delight yourself in the Lord, and He shall give you the desires of your heart."

She had been faithful to pass on the baton of service, the mantle of anointing, the shield of faith, and the torch of Pentecost. She had taken advantage of her time here on earth to **PASS IT ON.** She left us an example to live in such a way that we intentionally pass on to the next generation these essential tools for the next generation to live victoriously as they face their respective challenges. These are the priorities we need to focus on as we live our lives.

The following observations have stayed fresh on my mind. I would like to share them, having witnessed my mom's departure to her eternal home: First, after seeing Mom suffer, especially more on Friday and Saturday, I had been asking Eloy, my oldest brother, if there was a way all six siblings could make a corporate prayer. I just felt it was so essential. He said, "Yes, we could." It just so happened that no occasion had come where we were all together. Some would come, and some would go. However, one special moment on Saturday night, March 28, 2015, God's Spirit alerted me to the fact that all of our families, for the first time since I arrived on Tuesday, were now there represented. So, I asked Eloy—always wanting to respect his first-born right and leadership of the family—if we could pray together. I pondered on how, at this moment, here were the offspring of this wonderful union of Mom and Dad. God was preparing for her homegoing to heaven. He united us for this moment. He wanted to remind us that as we held hands in His presence to release Mom, we cannot forget that we are still a unit, because that is how He purposed it in His plans.

Eloy, so efficiently and with anointing, brought us together. He led us in a beautiful prayer, inspired by the Holy Spirit, in words that confirmed that there could be no doubt we were "in one accord." Jose, the third-born son, was not there, but symbolically he was there because his daughter, Vanessa, was there in that moment and represented him and his family. It was a beautiful, unforgettable experience that led us from there to pray for one another. May this linger and stand out in the chambers of mine and my siblings' memory to keep us connected by mail, email, texts, Facebook, FaceTime, and intentionally plan to unite for some times together now that Mom is gone. We belong together by God's divine plan, so we need to stay connected. We are all up in age, and any day God could call any of us home.

As of the writing of this book, all of us—six siblings—are 74–82 years of age. I am the youngest at 74, and my twin brothers are the oldest at 82. My brother, José, is 80; my sister, Sylvia, is 78; and my brother, Paul, is 77. To the glory of God, all of us, the six couples, have celebrated our 50th wedding anniversaries and still counting—from 53 years of marriage (my husband and me) to 59 years of marriage (my oldest twin brothers). That is not too common nowadays, but we saw the marriage vows kept till death did part our parents. As my siblings and I live on and as God grants us life, may we continue to be joined in love and communication. Distance doesn't really have to separate us, for it is up to us to take advantage of the marvelous means of communication and ways of connecting that advanced technology provides. When health and finances permit us to physically meet, that will be wonderful and refreshing! We love to pray together, sing together, laugh together, and play different instruments as we praise the Lord and reminisce about so many experiences. When we sing those songs and hymns, we remember our childhood.

Second, at some point on Saturday or Sunday, when Clarissa, my parents' first-born great-grandchild, came in, we joined in prayer at Mom's bedside. As I was with Clarissa and Mom and holding their hands, not sure why, I felt led to call Eloy and Anna to put their hands over Clarissa's and Mom's hands. As soon as I saw their hands together (Mom's, Clarissa's, Anna's, and Eloy's) atop one another, I sensed God's Holy Spirit speaking to me of how unique, significant, and special this was in the Kingdom and in God's plans for generations to come. For the last time, the four generations would be joined uniquely under God on this earth.

It is very significant that Mom represented her generation, Eloy (her firstborn) represented our generation of siblings, Anna (her first-born granddaughter) represented all the generation of grandchildren, and Clarissa (the first-born great-granddaughter) represented all the generation of the great-grandchildren.

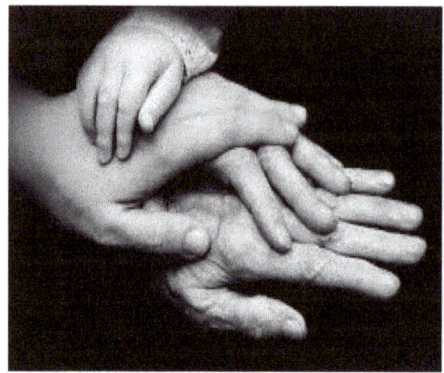

I was already in the middle of writing this book entitled *"PASS IT ON."* The Old Testament has much to say about passing on faith and its importance. Rest assured that the legacy of our grandparents' and parents' faith lives on in us because they were faithful to "Pass It On." We each have a window of time to pass on the faith. May we be found faithful. God is counting on us. May it not be said of any of our generations, as the Bible says in *Joshua,* that there arose a generation who knew not God.

In the hospice books, passing on to eternity was compared to the labor of childbirth. For me, childbirth labor pains were intense, and I thought when I had my firstborn child that my back would break in half. Labor pains in death can be intense too, and we witnessed it as Mother moaned and sighed. But just as with birth, once we see the fruit of our labor—our baby—the pains of childbirth are erased, and we get on with enjoying the new stage of parenting. As I thought about this, I reflected on the fact that, as the baby of the family, I was the last one of my siblings to be with her for her child-bearing labor. God granted that I was the last one present for her labor in death as she transitioned to her home in glory. As a song we sing reminds us:

"One glimpse of His sweet face, all sorrows will erase, so bravely run the race till we see Him."

She has no memory now, nor will she ever, of the suffering of this earth. She is getting on with her new life of rejoicing in the presence of God. The last words of that same song are what Mom did. She bravely ran the race, so now it is the challenge for each one of us to bravely run the race till we see Christ. We must model faith-walking for those who come behind us.

In *Joshua 4:21,* Joshua reminds us:

"In the future when your children ask you…"

Our children will ask—let's be ready to tell them, "This is where God did a great thing for us." Then in *Joshua 4:24* we read God's purpose in the miracle of the Israelites crossing the Jordan on dry ground:

"He did this so all the peoples of the earth might know that the hand of the Lord is powerful, and so you might always fear the Lord your God forever" *(NIV).*

It is a God-given mandate throughout the Bible to pass on the faith to each subsequent generation. We are each, individually, tasked with the great responsibility of relating, sharing, conveying the Word of God, the Love of God, the Truth of God, the Fear of God, and the Power of God.

On the following pages are included the lyrics to a song I wrote some years ago while preparing a sermon with this book title, and as I pondered the idea of writing a book with this title.

PASS IT ON

Words and Music by Doris Loida Espinoza- Recorded this in 2010

     Can be heard on You Tube

Introduction: Words and Actions, let us PA**SS IT ON**.

1

A **BATON** is handed from one generation to the other,
As we continue on this race that leads to eternity.
Oh, how critical is the moment when the **BATON** is handed over.
Let us not drop it, so those who come behind can grasp it
And run the race before them.

Chorus 1 – BATON of SERVICE

PASS IT ON, PASS IT ON, that **BATON** of dedicated service,
PASS IT ON.

God is counting on us to **PASS IT ON.**
We are here for such a time as this.
And we must not remain silent.
With words and actions, Let's **PASS IT ON.**

2

The **MANTLE** is a symbol of God's service and anointing.
And it is passed as generations walk by our side.
Experiencing the Power of God, the Miraculous. and Supernatural.
Then when it is our time to go, the **MANTLE** will fall on them
And with it a double portion of God's Spirit.

Chorus 2 – MANTLE OF ANOINTING

PASS IT ON, PASS IT ON,
the **MANTLE of ANOINTING,** please
PASS IT ON.

God is counting on us to **PASS IT ON.**
We are here for such a time as this,
And we must not remain silent,
With words and actions, let 's **PASS IT ON.**

3

God is calling us to take up our **SHIELD.**

Our **SHIELD of FAITH** with which we will extinguish the fiery darts of the evil one.

And then He orders us to **PASS the SHIELD** to the future generations.

So, they can believe for miracles and protect themselves from those darts meant for their destruction.

Chorus 3 – SHIELD OF FAITH

PASS IT ON, PASS IT ON,

The **SHIELD of UNWAVERING FAITH,**

PASS IT ON.

God is counting on us to **PASS IT ON.**
Oh, we are here for such a time as this
And we must not remain silent.
With words and actions, let's **PASS IT ON.**

4

The **TORCH OF PENTECOSTAL POWER** was given by God's Spirit to empower us. Old men will dream dreams and young men visions will see. It burns within and cannot be silenced.

Our sons and daughters must see, hear and know

God's Spirit will be poured on them and on all flesh, and they will prophecy.

Chorus 4 – TORCH OF PENTECOST

PASS IT ON, PASS IT ON, that **TORCH of Pentecostal Power**

PASS IT ON. God is counting on us to **PASS IT ON.**

We are here for such a time as this, and we must not remain silent.

With words and actions, let's **PASS IT ON.**

I have expressed my heart's passion for those who come behind me to experience the love of God, the power of God, the glory of God, and to walk in the purpose and ministry God has destined for their lives. I have entrusted the truths, lessons, and sermons God is giving and has given me to many, and I have found fulfillment in seeing many of those individuals be lifted by God to high callings and dedicated service. **PASS IT ON.**

I have been blessed to live to see their ministries flourish or see them in their professions touching lives. I will dedicate myself to this as long as there is life and breath left in me. I love the way the apostle Paul expressed it so clearly in 2 Timothy 2:2:

"And the things you have heard me say in the presence of many witnesses entrust to reliable people who will also be qualified to teach others."

Knowing we have a limited time to carry out our ministry, our work, our assignment should motivate us to intentionally prepare others. Like Paul, each of us has a Timothy. Paul recognized the value of training and developing Timothy into a faithful servant to whom he could pass on the baton of service. As God, through His Holy Spirit, enabled Paul to be alert to that, He will enable us to see the potential in those who work with us.

Paul carefully selected Timothy to work with him. Led by the Holy Spirit, we too will be selecting individuals by God's divine plan, providence, and direction to work with us—individuals with a teachable spirit like Timothy's. Remember, we do not minimize our legacy by teaching them all we can and engaging them in ministry opportunities with us. Instead, like Paul, may we ensure that the passion that motivates us to serve, the principles we stand for, and the anointing God has upon our lives will resound to glorify God for generations to come.

I share an experience I had as the principal of a Christian school and a director of a state-certified childcare facility. I had just become the director in a setting where I stepped in to take this position/ministry but had to leave for a trip to the Holy Land. New myself in this kind of service and ministry, I needed to find someone who could be in charge there while I was gone those two weeks. I prayed for God to lead me and show someone whom I could trust with this enormous task and heavy responsibility.

One morning in a church service, with that heavy on my heart and in prayer, I opened my eyes. To my surprise, everyone in that church service seemed to become a blur, and only one face was clear. I wondered what was happening, when I felt God clearly speak to my spirit — "She is the one, she is the one you can trust while you are out." It was a lady from our church named Leticia Mata, whom we lovingly call Sister Letty.

After service, I spoke to her and asked if she would be willing to do my job while I was gone. I trained her in the little I had learned up to that time. She did not know what it entailed, but she said, "Yes, Sister, anything I can do to help, I am willing to do"— and so began a mentorship. When I got back from the Holy Land, she continued to work. Together we worked and organized things in that office and childcare facility. Three years later, it was time to pass the baton to someone whom I trusted—she loved children, she had been willing to learn, and do all tasks I asked her to carry out. I would have her shadow me as I did the many duties that job/ministry entails. I left to work on my master's degree, and she became the director of the childcare facility and principal of the Christian school. Now, I would be working under her supervision for a few hours while I worked on my master's degree. She became my boss.

That was a little over ten years ago. I am still working as her assistant, part-time. I marvel at her leadership skills, wisdom, and expertise in childcare. God called her to this. It is a heavy responsibility that she carries with sensitivity and diligence. What an incredible journey in ministry this has been. To witness the wisdom God has given her and the abilities to lead these past ten years is rewarding and fulfilling. Now reverse mentoring is taking place as I learn from her.

Cassie, who I mentioned, earlier in the chapter of Passing the Baton of Service for being willing to take the baton of service, is Sister Letty's daughter. I get to see her dedication to mentor, teach, and prepare her son, Rene, for life. She is now a school counselor and impacts thousands of lives. I have seen her receive honors, awards and accolades for her excellent work with children and youth. Among those awards is the prestigious Crest Award of Texas Excellence in Counseling. She has also been named Counselor of the Month several times.

I realize now how God, in this journey, has given me the opportunity to mentor a mom and her daughters-two generations. She has another daughter, Lorraine Mata, whom I have the privilege of motivating, inspiring in her walk with the Lord, and praying with her and for her as she faces new opportunities, endeavors, and challenges. Lorraine has a daughter, Nevaiah

Grace--now about 7 or 8 years old. I have the privilege of teaching, mentoring, and pouring my love, knowledge and experience into her. I get to teach her God's Word, help her learn scriptures, guide her to sing unto the Lord, and more. Sis. Letty also has a son, Joe Christopher Mata, who married Rachelle Ochoa. They have two daughters, Truly and Mercy. By long distance and because of technology I have been blessed to disciple them through our lessons live on Facebook, and I have shared my recordings with them. One of their favorite songs I have recorded is "Christian Cowgirl." That can be heard on You Tube. Interestingly, their mom, Rachelle, used to attend our camps and was in our Girls Ministries clubs as a child and young lady. That makes three generations, God is giving me the privilege and honor to touch and **PASS IT ON.**

I say all this to convey that we don't only touch or mentor the generation behind us, but we impact future generations. God is amazing at orchestrating these plans and opportunities for mentoring and impacting these and many generations to come.

Longevity in a place unfolds opportunities to see the ways God fulfills His plans of generations preparing future generations. We have pastored at Templo Emanuel for 40 years. It is such a beautiful and rewarding experience seeing multiple generations rise up to leadership as God has honored us with the privilege to teach and prepare them.

In the Girls Ministries Discipleship Program, after 3 years of mentoring, discipleship, and dedicated study, girls are crowned Honor Stars—a great accomplishment. I am blessed that I have had the privilege of discipling and crowning my daughter, Dina, and 4 of my granddaughters: Rosio, Kiara, Sofía, and Isela Roiz. Plans are to crown my youngest granddaughter, Briza, next year. I have been discipling her for two years.

On the local church level, it has been my joy over these 40 years to disciple, train, mentor and crown several moms and years later, their daughters. Among those are: Teresa Rios Valadez and Selah- Teresa is now a Licensed Nurse Practitioner-Board Certified (FNP-BC); Melinda Jimenez Castillo and Elizabeth— Melinda is a school librarian and our Children's Pastor at Templo Emanuel; Dina and her 4 girls-Dina is a high school Language Arts teacher and assists in different areas of ministry in the church, but mostly in Praise and Worship. On a district level, I am now crowning the fourth generation of Honor Stars. Oh, the joy of serving in this ministry on the local level for over 40 years, on the district level for over 37 years.

Each one of us, like Elijah, has an Elisha—a successor that we have the privilege and responsibility to mentor and prepare. There may even be more than one. God has ways of making this happen as we walk in obedience and invite others to team up with us. We are not limited to touching, impacting, or preparing just one, but instead, God can use us to impact many others who will rise up to serve the Master to meet the need of their time. Oh, that there be more willing vessels like Elisha who are willing to pursue God's call and assignment, willing to humble themselves to serve, and to submit. Then again, Lord, may more servants like Elijah rise up who will be graced by Your Spirit to look beyond the ministry You are using us in to see beyond and humble ourselves for the sake of the next generations. Help us pass on the mantle of anointing!

There are families in our times, as there always have been, who can look to Eunice and Lois as examples—that we cannot let time pass by without instilling biblical principles in our children from infancy. Let's not be parents and grandparents who waited too long, then it was too late to spare them heartache and pain that could have been avoided had we taught them God's Word and passed on to them a shield of faith from their infant, toddler, and childhood years, and followed through into their youth and adult years. The shield of faith will serve as their protection against the fiery darts of the evil one launched to destroy them. With faith they will experience the miraculous, the glorious, the supernatural, and the amazing! They will live and walk by faith and not by sight.

We want our children saved, anointed, baptized in the Holy Spirit, serving with passion and prepared with the shield of faith to protect any area of their minds, their bodies, their emotions, their hearts, and their spirits whenever and however the enemy attacks with fiery darts and force. Let's ensure they are ready when those fiery darts of doubt, discouragement, questions on their identity, and addictions that the enemy wants to enslave them with come.

Let's Pass on the Shield of Faith! We can! We must! We will!!

Like Peter, we all have many on whom we are having an impact—who can and will embrace the truths of Scripture and will long for the power the torch of Pentecost imparts: that enables one to serve, to witness, to be obedient, to be bold, and to overcome. Lord, help us pass on that torch of Pentecost, here and there, and everywhere! May we be filled with the Holy Spirit and fire! May we walk in the Spirit and live in the Spirit. Oh, that the gifts of the Spirit will be operating in our lives, creating a thirst and a longing for the torch of Pentecost in those whom we teach and mentor. It's the power of the Holy Spirit continually burning in our lives that pushes us to speak boldly and share salvation's story so all may know.

As an old hymn we sing in Pentecostal churches expresses, may our constant prayer be: **"Oh Lord, send the fire just now, and baptize everyone."**

Let's ensure faith in God will be passed on to future generations. Use whatever means to accomplish this. Let's be honest to express to those close to us how serious and intentional we are that our children know and serve God. Let's intentionally pray for them and with them. Let's bring the family altar—with devotional time to worship God and hear from God—back to our homes. Let's sing and make music with them. Let the truths of precious hymns and contemporary music penetrate their hearts and minds. Sing on all occasions. Instill a love for music, and they will remember those lyrics and melodies when celebration times or hard times come, because you took time to make music in your home.

Then, let's cook their favorite meals and take advantage of those times around the table to laugh and converse in those eye-to-eye, heart-to-heart conversations. Those times at the table, tasting my parents' and my siblings' delectable meals, laughing with one another, and talking about anything and everything have left unforgettable memories in the chambers of my mind. They still provoke smiles and laughter today as I reminisce about those times. In tough times I remember the words to songs that brought us strength and comfort as children and in our youth.

I am so thankful for all those—too many to name—who have left footprints for me to follow in my faith walk, in my ministry, and in my education. Some of you reading this book right now may never know how you impacted my life. Theirs—and your—footprints have guided me to help me live out God's plans and purposes for my life. I want to leave footprints for my family, friends, co-workers, and mentees.

May all of us leave footprints that will guide those who come behind us. We are also leaving our **fingerprint** on so many lives—an impression, an inspiration, a mark. I can't leave anyone's fingerprint but mine, because fingerprints are unique to each individual. Your fingerprint is valuable. Let it mark someone's life.

My husband, Dino, shared a thought recently in a weekly devotional in our community newspaper which bears repeating here:

Fingerprints are unique and important. Before we became aware of their value, our parents would admonish us: "Don't touch that—you'll leave your fingerprints." They were correct—after playing outside, our dirty or sweaty hands would leave marks on tables and doors.

Today, we have the technology that affirms the value of fingerprints. They are the impressions of our fingers that give us a personal identification. It is interesting that each person has a personal set of fingerprints. Beyond the visible fingerprint, each one of us can also leave a special fingerprint or impression on others. As we connect with family, friends, or work colleagues—we leave our fingerprint of respect, kindness, compassion, and love.

Our vocabulary, attitudes, and actions are a personal set of fingerprints. Just as each fingerprint is unique—you and I are also unique. Consider this thought: **What is my life's fingerprint that touches others?**

Yes, it's our turn now to make a lasting mark. Will we step up to the plate? Will we take our turn to bat? Will we impact those whom God places in our path? Will we make a home run like Esther did when it was her turn to bat? Let's step up to the challenge. God is counting on us.

Only one life, and so soon it will pass. Let's take our turn, and let's be the ones that make a difference!

As with Esther, God knows that you and I have come to our place of influence in this specific time in history—His perfect timing, **"for such a time as this."** Just like Esther got to that place in the palace to fulfill God's plan for His people, so you and I are here now to impact this and the generations that come behind us.

I say, **Yes, Lord, I'll take my place in the unfolding of Your plans. Yes, Lord, I will PASS IT ON—the Shield of Faith, the Baton of Service, the Mantle of Anointing, and the Torch of Pentecost.** I will strive to ensure faith in God will be passed on to future generations.

Will you commit to this, as well?

IT'S OUR TURN!

We have a biblical mandate from God to see to it that the next generation hears about the mighty acts of God.

Our goal in passing it on is to raise up children and young people—yes, generations of persons fully surrendered to Jesus, filled with the Holy Spirit, and fulfilling the Great Commission to spread the good news of salvation—**PASS IT ON!**

Judges 2:10 – "And all that generation also were gathered to their fathers. And there arose another generation after them who did not know the Lord or the work that He had done for Israel."

Here we have a clear, vivid example of a generation that failed to tell—a generation who failed to **PASS IT ON**—a generation with an absence of godly fathers and leaders.

It is never too late to change a pattern and to start a legacy of godly influence Let it not be repeated that a generation rose up after us who did not know the Lord.

Tell it! Share it! Read it! Teach it! Sing it! By all means, let's PASS IT ON!

Eli, Ashley, Rosio, Grandma Loida, Grandpa Dino, Kiara, Dina, Mateo, Mi Timoteo; Sofia, then front row: Jadon, Isela, Levi, Briza

Grandparents, Doris Loida Espinoza and Bernardino (Dino) Espinoza Intentionally Passing on the Baton of Service, the Mantle of Anointing, the Shield of Faith, and the Torch of Pentecost.

Our 8 Grandchildren: Back row: Levi, Rosio, Jadon;
Front Row: Isela, Briza, Sofía, Kiara (Kiki) and Mateo, mi Timoteo.

To them and others: I will be faithful to PASS ON: The BATON of Service, the MANTLE of Anointing, the SHIELD of Faith and the TORCH of Pentecost.

Selected Bibliography

Clinton, Tim, Chap Clark, and Joshua Stab. *Counseling Teenagers.* Grand Rapids, Michigan: Baker Book, 2010.

Crabtree, Charles T., "The Secret of Happiness,*"* *Pentecostal Evangel,*(Springfield, MO) September 16, 2007.

Garland, Diana R. *Family Ministry: Comprehensive Guide.* Downers Grove, IL: Intervarsity Press, 2012.

Hahn, Laura. "Too Much Texting? *"*. *Good Housekeeping,* December 2009. 127.

Hill, John L.,H.W. Tribble, and Kyle M. Yates, *Old Testament Biographies,* Nashville, Tennessee: Broadman Press, 1935

Norris, Robert. "A Spiritual Father," *Charisma.* July 2014.

O'Connell, Ashli "The Right Way," *Pentecostal Evangel* .(Springfield, MO) March 30, 2014.

Reddout, David, "All Generations" *"All Generations, Sermon Outlines,* (Springfield, MO) 2010.

Riccioth, Giuseppe. *PAUL The Apostle.* Milhuakee: the Bruce Publishing Company

Richards, Sue and Larry, *Every Woman in the Bible.* Nashville.,TN: Thomas Nelson Publishers, 1999.

Stephens, William H., *Elijah".* Wheaton, Illinois: Tyndale House Publishers, 1976.

Titus, Devi, and Marilyn Weiher, *The Home Experience* .Korea, Living Smart Resources, a division of Kingdom Global Ministries, 2006.

Reflections For Deeper Individual or Group Study

Introduction

To what season of the year would you compare the present stage in your life and why?

_____

_____

_____

_____

Read, meditate and ponder on the following verses that instruct us to pass on faith and truths of God's power, provision, and protection to the generations that come behind us. Write a personal reflection on each one. Use your favorite version of the Bible. If you are in a group study, share your reflections and emphasize the importance God places on parents and elders. God is counting on us. God is intentional on working through generations. Let's be intentional.

Deuteronomy 32.7: Remember the days of old; consider the generations long past. Ask your father, and he will tell you, your elders, and they will explain to you. (NIV)

_____

_____

_____

_____

Exodus 13.14: "In days to come (in the future), when your son asks you, 'What does this mean?' say to him, 'With a mighty hand the LORD brought us out of Egypt, out of the house of slavery. ' Read all chapter 13, then write what this means to you personally.

_____

_____

_____

_____

Joshua 4.21-22: And he said to the people of Israel, "When your children ask their fathers in times to come, 'What do these stones mean?' then you shall let your children know, 'Israel passed over this Jordan on dry ground.' Read Joshua Chapters 4 and 5. Discuss the miracle of crossing the Jordan and answer the question: Why did God do this miracle, according to Joshua 4:24? Write this verse which answers this question:

_____

_____

_____

_____

Psalm 71.18: So even to old age and gray hairs, O God, do not forsake me, until I proclaim your might to another generation, your power to all those to come. This is the Psalmists prayer. Write your own prayer in reference to your desire to "Pass It On."

_____

_____

_____

_____

Read entire Psalm 78- 78:6 [...] so the next generation would know them (know what?) even the children yet to be born, and that they, in turn, will tell them to their children. (NIV) Write a short reflection on this Psalm.

_____

_____

_____

_____

Psalm 145.4: One generation shall commend(praise) your works to another, and shall declare your mighty acts. (NIV) Write at least one praise report or mighty act you can share and declare of God's mighty acts. (Praises will carry the truth to other generations.)

_____

_____

_____

_____

Add any additional verses you can find or insight on this topic of "Pass It On."

_____

_____

_____

_____

****

Let's keep our minds focused on God's intention then and now.

****

Chapter 1: Don't Drop It – Pass It On - The Importance of Mentoring

Have you witnessed what you think is dropping or disregarding something of high value by the present generation? In what areas?

_____

_____

_____

_____

What can you do to restore what has been dropped/disregarded since it is valuable to you?

_____

_____

_____

_____

Write down a precious memory or two, a commendable work or moving story and its value to you that would make you want to pass it on to the future generations.

_____

_____

_____

_____

Ponder on the question posed in this chapter: What am I doing to fulfill God's idea and plan to mentor someone?

_____

_____

_____

_____

What can I do?

_____

_____

_____

_____

How do you perceive technology and social medias are limiting or affecting the communication between generations and opportunities to foster passing it on?

_____

_____

_____

_____

****

Let's keep our minds focused on God's intention then and now.

****

Whether you are young or old, rich or poor, you have eyes watching you and learning from you.

Chapter 2: Paul - Pass it on – The Baton of Service

Paul likens the journey of faith as a race. Considering that, where are you in the race of faith walking? (Just beginning, a few years in, many years in) _____ Give the date you started this walk _____

Write a short reflection of how you began this race. Who or what contributed to you deciding to begin this race of following Jesus? What was the setting?

_____

_____

_____

_____

Paul also likens this journey from earth to glory as a fight. He said, "I have fought the good fight." He shares the victories of serving Christ. Write one of the victories Timothy witnessed.

_____

_____

_____

_____

Now you write a victory or two that you have experienced in your journey of life.

_____

_____

_____

_____

Paul also shared the hardships and difficulties of life with Timothy. Write at least one of those difficulties that Timothy witnessed.

_____

_____

_____

_____

Write about/share about a difficulty or hardship that you battled/experienced in your life and how God brought you through.

_____

_____

_____

_____

Chapter 3: Elijah and Elisha – Pass it on – The Mantle of Anointing

Find (individually or as a group) and list and/or discuss some of the miracles in which God used Elijah and some of the miracles in which God used Elisha.

_____

_____

_____

_____

Write your own definition of a mantle of anointing.

_____

_____

_____

_____

Elisha repeated a lot of what his master did, but as we read, he had his own mission and manner of carrying it out uniquely. Choose one person you have observed ministering. What are some of their practices or characteristics of their devotional life would you like to repeat. Share that with someone.

_____

_____

_____

_____

When a mantle of anointing, by God's divine order, falls on us, it is not just for us to repeat some of those things we admire in our mentors, but to take up the journey or the task where they left off.

Write a few things you would like to see happen or things you feel God has been leading you to do or pursue that you would like to implement as you are moving into new avenues of life or ministry.

_____

_____

_____

_____

Our childhood and teen years are a time of learning and preparing ourselves for the future that God and your elders have been preparing you for. What do you, as of now, perceive God is leading you to? Elaborate on a separate sheet of paper if needed-

_____

_____

_____

_____

Chapter 4: Lois and Eunice - Pass it on – The Shield of Faith

In Ephesians 6, the Bible depicts faith as a SHIELD and part of the armor of God. Read Ephesians 6. Write verse 16:

_____

_____

_____

_____

Write a personal reflection or discuss with someone the content and meaning of this scripture.

_____

_____

_____

_____

Mention or write the title of a book that has influenced your faith. If in a group, some of you may want to share book titles after commenting on some.

_____

_____

_____

_____

The Bible says that faith comes by hearing, and hearing of the WORD. Write your thoughts on this:

_____

_____

_____

_____

Are there ways to follow faith on a device or smart phone and live out your faith?

_____

_____

_____

_____

In a world of technology, what are your thoughts on faith-building and living by faith?

_____

_____

_____

_____

What is the best thing about being a believer and walking this life by faith?

_____

_____

_____

_____

What is the most influential story in the Bible for you? Write about it or discuss it.

_____

_____

_____

_____

Chapter 5: Peter -Pass it on – The Torch of Pentecost

Read Chapter 2 of Acts--then ponder on, write, and discuss the chapter. What amazes you most in this chapter that describes what happened on the Day of Pentecost?

_____

_____

_____

_____

Write the words of Acts 2:17.

_____

_____

_____

_____

Try to memorize it (Individually or as a group). Write about what you perceive about this promise for you, your children and grandchildren.

_____

_____

_____

_____

Write Acts 2:39

_____

_____

_____

_____

For whom is this promise?

_____

_____

_____

_____

Believe it, receive it, walk in it!

PASS IT ON!

Prayer: Lord, I surrender to you completely. Immerse me in the river of your Holy Spirit. I come before you with an open heart and deep desire to be filled daily with the Holy Spirit. I choose to believe in and walk in your promises. Empower me to be the witness/the vessel you need me to be in your Kingdom and to **PASS IT ON**! Write or share your thoughts on how the Torch of Pentecost makes the difference in a Christian's life.

_____

_____

_____

_____

Chapter 6: How Can This Generation Ensure Faith in God Will Be Passed on to Future Generations?

Choose two of the six ways given or one God has given you to ensure faith is passed on to the next generations.

List the first way you have chosen, then write about how you will follow through. If you are in a group study, share it with your group.

_____

_____

_____

_____

List the second way you have chosen, then write about how you will follow through. If you are in a group study, share it with your group.

_____

_____

_____

_____

Read, write and try to memorize Deuteronomy 6:6 where Moses instructs and highlights the responsibility that each generation has to model and teach faith that is integrated into their everyday living, into their plans for the future, into their conversations and their story telling. Write that verse here

_____

_____

This is one way the generations behind us will have a firm foundation of faith to last them and be lived out. Discuss how to do this and what Moses meant.

Write a personal reflection of some thoughts, ideas, and challenges that have come to your mind as you have read this book, and write your own short summary of what you are inspired to do. What has God spoken to your heart?

God bless you, inspire you, and empower you as you pursue what we have been instructed to do and what we have seen modeled for us through biblical examples. To young people, I encourage you to find people you see walking confidently, trusting God, and pursuing excellence. Shadow them. Let them know you are willing to learn. Submit to their counsel. God will honor your efforts and willingness to learn. He will open doors of opportunities you could have never dreamed. Ephesians 3:20 remind us: "Now to Him who is able to do immeasurably more than all we ask or imagine, according to His power that is at work within us." (NIV)

Acknowledgements

My thanks to my siblings, Eloy, Lee Roy, Jose, Sylvia and Paul. As the youngest child in our Padilla family, I learned so much from them. I gleaned from their example. Their support of my endeavors in life have pushed me forward to accept new challenges and do my best. Jose and Sylvia initially helped in proof reading and cheering me on to write my heart's passion. Their pursuit of excellence led me to strive for nothing less of excellence. Anything that I have accomplished in musical compositions and recordings is to the credit of my talented brothers and my sister. They know what a miracle God performed in taking my dreams since a child, while they patiently listened, advised, and prayed for me. May the words written in this book also be a tribute to our parents, Jose Leandro Padilla and Abedulia Martinez Padilla and their siblings, my aunts and uncles, who cared enough to give us their best and to Pass on the Baton of Service, the Mantle of Anointing, the Shield of Faith, and the Torch of Pentecost.

I thank my Superintendent, Rev. Eddie De La Rosa, for reviving in me the desire to finish this book, which I had started so many years ago, but life happens, and I had put it away. Out of the blue one day he said, "you can have a book by next year, right?" I told him I had one started and would go home, pray and try to finish it. One year later, I finished it. Thanks for your leadership and for believing in me.

I thank all the guys and gals who accepted the challenge to go with us on missions trips and minister in the United States and in foreign countries. We have been blessed to see you develop in ministries you never dreamed, but that God had ordained for you. Keep fulfilling the Great Commission, its's dear to God's heart.

A BIG thanks to all who have worked with my husband and me in our pastorates, in Children's, Youth, Girls, and Women's Ministries. What a joy it has been. God granted us so many wonderful experiences. Thank you for teaching me and for letting me lead and teach you. Together God taught us the power of prayer, the power of praise, the power of trust, and His faithfulness. He continues to fulfill His promises. I cherish our camps/conventions/retreats and other events we planned together or attended together that required so much work and dedication, but we saw and continue to see the fruit of our labor --So many children, young people, girls. men and women are saved, filled with the Holy Spirit, pursuing ministry -- others are already in varied ministries because of what we planned together under the guidance of the Holy Spirit. On my behalf I repeat to you Paul's words to the Philippians: "Whatever you have learned or received or heard from me—put it into practice. And the God of peace will be with you. (Philippians 4:9).

I am thankful for Isela Martinez, Frances Mendoza, Fran De Leon, Gertrude Garza, Mary Helen Lozano, Zilpa Alfaro Gutierrez, Liz Aguirre, and the late Charlotte Garza--together we worked for several years in Girls Ministries on the district level to cultivate the future generations and to pass it on. You gave yourselves fully--your labor has not been in vain. (I Corinthians 15:58).

I want to thank the following leaders, who in these past several years, have walked beside me - supporting me in all the responsibilities that the ministries I was involved in entailed. I delegated duties and they diligently carried those out with excellence. Here in this mentorship is embodied my passion for cultivating and preparing the future generations. These gals are ready to run with a heart for God and with experience and skills God has and is granting them as they accept assignments in His Kingdom and in His timing. They are here for such a time as this. My desire all along has been to pass to them and to all those who have been working alongside us: The Baton of Service, the Mantle of Anointing, the Shield of Faith, and the Torch of Pentecost. They are Janie Gonzalez, Carolina Balderas, Keila Sanchez, and Yolanda Rodriguez.

I want to thank María Elena Nuño Rodriguez for partnering with me to lead and prepare those who are taking and will take our place. Your integrity, consistency, and dedication to cultivating the future generations have impacted my life. We press on in Jesus' name, believing and thanking him for the promise in his Word in Psalm 92:14: "They shall still bear fruit in old age; they shall be fresh and fruitful." We are living out that promise as we move forward in Jesus' name, and we are thankful for our health and the doors God opens to continue using us to fulfill His plans and purposes.

I would like to thank Esther Garza, an outstanding and inspiring leader, for her part in helping with this mission to prepare the future generations. The scholarships offered through Women's Ministries speak volumes of your commitment to missions and cultivating the future generations.

I am including some questions I posed to some teenagers in hopes that there can be a blending of the generations as we pursue the task to "**Pass It On**." May God help us glean from these responses what the present generation is going through, is asking from us, expecting of us, and what they are willing to do. Let's not underestimate their expectations nor their desires and willingness. Let's be there for them and with God's help prepare them to live and lead our communities, our nation, our world, and the Church of Jesus Christ.

If you are a young person, perhaps you can ponder on these questions and come up with answers of your own that you can share with the generations before you. What we can all glean and learn from their answers is that they want to learn, grow, and serve. They want our presence. We can perceive how they enjoy relaxing family times indoors or outdoors, and how they feel those times are becoming less and less. They want to connect with us, but we need to intentionally build relationships with them so they can trust us, follow us, and learn from us. Their answers and comments remind us of our task and assignment: **PASS IT ON**! ---Let's do it!

A Young Generation Speaks Out

Question # 1: What is a favorite childhood memory?

Answers: My favorite childhood memory is when I would play outside my neighborhood with all my friends. We thrived on being outdoors and close friendships developed that are cherished beyond childhood. We were healthy children. It seems children today are not experiencing those out-door, enjoyable playtimes.

Having cookouts with my mom and brother. The aroma in the air, the good food, the relaxation of being outdoors have a way of imprinting those special times in my memory.

Going to church every Sunday with my whole family, showing my parents what I made/did in our Children's Church Chapel and eating with everyone after service. Eating together at services or after services seemed to be more prevalent then compared to now, however, those were special times to talk, laugh, and learn. Families connected and built lasting friendships during those meal times together.

My favorite childhood memory is outdoor barbeques with my family and relatives. We had such a good time relaxing and laughing. We don't do it anymore. The aroma in the air, the connecting, the laughing I experienced has left me longing for more times like that.

My favorite childhood memory is playing sports.

My favorite childhood memory is when my family and me went on a summer vacation.

My favorite childhood memory is when I was 11 years old. I saved up enough change in a bucket to make $120, and I bought my first kitten. I bought him and all his supplies on my own.

Another said, "The older generations could help other children and young people experience the joy and fulfillment of working for something on our own, instead of just buying everything for us. There is fulfillment in earning or saving that my generation needs to experience. Help us and encourage us to earn on our own and to learn how to save. The thrill of buying something you earned and worked for is, indeed, rewarding."

Question # 2 – Do you think technology has changed the way people relate? If so, how?

Technology has, definitely, changed how people relate, making it easier to connect across distances, but it also reduces face-to-face interactions.

Yes, I think technology has changed the way people relate because so many people now don't go outside to explore, they rather be on their phones. People walk outdoors less and lose advantages of what the outdoors offer in fun and fitness, valuing more the scrolling and spending hours on their phones or electronic devices.

Yes, I think technology has changed the way people relate because in these times people can share their interest and opinions with each other, not just in their communities, and nations, but all around the world. This is amazing!

Yes, I think technology has good and bad impacts on people now because social media can be positive and negative---and social media is BIG in our generation. It takes a lot of discipline to try to stay off of our phones. I like it, but it tires me out.

Question # 3: What is the biggest challenge you feel you are facing in your life now?

Answers: Right now, a big challenge is staying focused and managing time effectively with so many distractions.

The biggest challenge I am currently facing is making meaningful and deep connections with others. Often times, due to people being more accessible online, being replaced or ignored becomes common.

The biggest challenge I am facing in my life now is deciding whether to graduate early or not, but either way, God has a plan for all of us—and we just have to trust it.

I think my biggest challenge is my emotions. I struggle to communicate how I feel and how to react to certain situations. But I will say, praying has helped me a lot.

I think living with only one of my parents has been draining and hard sometimes, also because my parents aren't on the best terms 99 % of the time, but I am still trying to trust in the Lord's plan and trying to be patient.

Question # 4: What would you like the older generation to know and understand about your generation?

Answers: I wish the older generation understood how much pressure we feel to succeed and how different the job market is now.

I would like the older generation to understand that the younger generation should not be rushed to grow up. Forced or sped-up maturity has only affected me negatively. I feel that it has robbed me of my innocence in some way.

It would be great if the generation before me could create more opportunities for young people to get involved in decision making.

I would like the older generation to know that they lived life in a good way—no technology, just everyone being with each other. Living undistracted and connected person-to-person, heart-to-heart--not connected by superficial friendships on social media, texts, etc. must have been special and something I long for.

I wish that the generation before me would set the right example and understand that our generation does want role models we can follow and imitate. I would like them to know and understand that it is okay to be yourself and you don't have to do what others do just to fit in.

I would like them to understand that we grew up very differently and we are not going to experience life the same way they did.

I would like them to understand that being a kid nowadays is different. It doesn't seem to be as carefree for us today as it seems it was for past generations. The fears we have to face and the precautions we have to take nowadays is troubling. The pressures that weigh us down often bring anxiety.

Question # 5: What would you like those older than you to teach you?

Answers: I would love help on how to navigate life.

Please teach us how to be disciplined in a world with so many distractions. I know we do not have self-control and I want to learn that.

I would love to learn more about their experiences and wisdom from different times.

I wish the generation before me would invest more of their time into becoming teachers. The lack of teachers has significantly affected mine and other students' abilities to learn efficiently.

I would like those that are older than me to teach me about the time before me. Personal experience with history is valuable.

I wish this generation before me would help my generation grow a better relationship with and become closer to God, because God is so good and powerful. He can change anyone's life for the better if we trust him and grow closer to Him. I would want the older generation to be like they were back then in their generation—happy and outdoors a lot, and model it for us.

Just to give us advice on trusting and being patient as we grow to be a woman or man of God. Sometimes we feel we won't amount to much. We want encouragement and to be taught practical ways to muddle through our teen age years.

I would want those older than me to teach me the things that I need to know in life to survive, to cope, to thrive, and to succeed.

Question # 6: Do you feel comfortable asking older persons questions? If not, why not?

Answers: If I know them, yes, I feel comfortable.

Sometimes, depends on the person and how comfortable I am in the environment or with the person.

I feel comfortable asking older people questions because they often have valuable insights.

I am often more comfortable asking older people questions rather than my peers.

Yes, Of course.

I don't feel comfortable asking older people questions.

Question # 7: Are you willing to be taught, mentored, and be accountable to someone of the older generation? Why or why not?

Answers: Yes, I would be willing to be taught because I want to live the way they lived back then when no one had to worry about anyone judging, being mean or caring what anyone else says. Bullying is real and it is ugly. Hearts are broken and emotions crushed. The standards and principles taught and practiced before minimized opportunities for others to be mean. There was a lot more focus on character building and respect for authority and one another. I would love our generation to be taught and required to enforce those godly principles too, so we can put them into practice. Nobody seems to have time to teach us and enforce that, yet it is expected of us. Yes, although we have and are experiencing life differently, it does not hurt to take advice from others.

Yes, I would want to grow to be a responsible and trustworthy woman/man of God.

No, I am not willing to be taught, mentored and be accountable to someone of the older generation.

I believe the message of this book relates, in more ways than one, that God is serious about the need of older generations to teach/cultivate the future generations. It is and has always been His plan.

While completing this book, I attended a gathering of ministerial families, which we call our District Council. It was the District Council of the Texas Gulf Hispanic District. The theme was: **"Preparing the Future Generations."** It resonated in my heart the divine assignment we have. I sensed deep in my spirit how timely the title of this book and the challenge to fulfill it is.

My last comments from the hearts and minds of young people are from a 12-year old boy, Santiago("Santi") Levi Rocha, who addressed all of us there on that theme. His words should stir us into action. If you are doing it, GREAT! However, if you are not investing time, money, energy, presence, and guidance to cultivate the future generations, please step up to the task and be intentional. His words:

"I do not doubt that God can do anything, however, I firmly believe that God is calling parents, leaders, and pastors to **be intentional** about raising and discipling the next generation. Just like me, there are many young people that God is calling and wants to raise up for His glory, but now, more than ever, we need our leaders to believe that we are "no ordinary children" and take a stand against the enemy's strategies."

LET'S DO IT INTENTIONALLY---------LET'S PASS IT ON!

Many of you, like myself, have had experiences that push you to ponder on the reality of eternity and on the truth that we cannot predict how much time we have on this earth. The following experience and others have taught me that **Life is Fragile** and must be handled with prayer. Experiences like this remind me of the urgency to **PASS IT ON** while I can. I want to close this book with this experience and open up the opportunity for you to reflect on similar experiences, though different, but that jolted you into looking at the things that really count—like faith, family, eternity and God's assignment to each of us to **PASS IT ON**. This gives every reader the opportunity to evaluate and prepare to **PASS IT ON**, not knowing how long we have to fulfill this assignment. I have entitled this reflection: **Life is Fragile – Handle with Prayer**.

LIFE IS FRAGILE –
Handle with Prayer

God Has an Assignment – Pass it on

One Monday in my reading of the Word and prayer, I had read the scripture in Isaiah 43:2: ***When you pass through the water, I will be with you; and through the rivers, they shall not overflow you, for I am the Lord, your God. When you walk(go) through the fire, you shall not be burned, nor shall the flame scorch. For I am the Lord, your God, the Holy One of Israel, your Savior.***

Throughout the week, I pondered on that portion of that Bible verse. I left home on a lovely day (Thursday, April 17, 2008) with expectations of a trip to Leakey, TX and back. Our first regional Women's Ministries retreat would be held at the lovely campground in two weeks. To my surprise, between La Pryor and Crystal City, I lost control of the vehicle I was driving.

My car sped to the opposite lane, facing the oncoming traffic. I saw vehicles coming toward me and tried to maneuver the steering wheel to avoid hitting them. I had no control over what was happening. I began to hit brush, trees, and then fence posts-one, two, three, four. I saw two telephone posts and was going directly toward them. I cried out, "Jesus." I found out later that miraculously the car actually sped between the two telephone posts. I finally hit a tree or post and my car began flips and turns in the air.

It finally fell with a crash and landed upside down. I was strapped inside still in my seat with my seatbelt fastened /locked and with my head hanging near the radio. I looked around, noticed I was alive and breathing, but had no way of getting out. The power windows were locked. The front windshield was completely shattered and covered with brush that was so high and completely blocking the windshield, so I could not see anything to the front of the car. I prayed, Jesus, please send your angels, and lay me on someone's heart." It seemed to me that about six minutes passed, when I heard voices around the vehicle.

I said, "Thank you, Jesus. Please let them get to me before it's too late." Soon the men whose voices I was hearing broke the window behind the driver's seat, and began conversing with me— trying to assess my condition. I told them, "I am okay, but please, get me out of here." They said, "we'll do our best." They could not get me out, nor could I release the seat belt. I was hanging upside down and trapped in the seat by my seatbelt.

Some men from a construction crew got together and broke the window on the driver's side to try to pry the seat away from the locked seat belt. When they did, I felt release from my neck, which had been bent to fit the small space between the caved-in ceiling/roof of my car that had been smashed with the final landing. God helped me keep calm. The men could still not get to me, so they broke the other windows. One or two of the men found a tool to cut my seatbelt. They asked if I could move. They figured that if, perhaps, I could move, I could try to maneuver my body to try to fit through a small opening near the back window on the passenger's side. I twisted and turned my body to fit through the very small space, and I began making my way to the only tiny opening of the car. Once I made it there, the men present pulled me out.

With my head and my upper body out, they helped me as I worked to get my thighs, legs, and feet out. Miraculously I was out. "Hallelujah, thank you, Jesus," I cried, and then I lifted both arms high toward the sky. Some passers-by said what impressed them is that I was on my knees with my hands up to the sky. I remember lifting my hands, but I do not remember kneeling down; however, that is what my normal reaction would be, so it must have been so if someone saw it. Who else could I thank for life, but God?

Those present immediately warned me to run far away from the car as a fire was blazing behind the car from sparks from my hits to the poles that had ignited the dry grass. When I finally sat on a dirt pile and looked at the up-side-down car, I could see a blazing fire about 20 feet high and spreading fast. I asked those around me to take a photo of that fire, as it would attest to the care and shelter of God's loving arms that embraced and enveloped me through this entire experience. Perhaps someone has those photos, I do not know. They assured me they had dispatched an ambulance, the fire department, and the police. How amazing, that God had already dispatched his angels.

I found out when I got home that night from the hospital that in Guatemala, a leader had sent out an email that morning to pray for Sister Doris Loida Espinoza, who would be their speaker in November for their girls' camp. She expressed that it was important to pray since now for her protection, for her health, and anointing to bring messages that would minister to the present needs of their girls. It was April and I would not be speaking till November, but God bless those who heeded to her call for prayer for me. I know God heard and my life was spared, for such a time as this.

The ambulance staff prepared me and put me on the stretcher. We began our ride to the Uvalde Memorial Hospital. I remember the beautiful young lady that God ordained to be the ambulance attendant for my incredible experience. She took my blood pressure and was surprised that my blood pressure was normal. Apparently, most accident victims' blood pressure rises due to the trauma and the panic that can overtake them in the midst of such circumstances. I remember her sharing that information and expression of surprise with the ambulance driver. I immediately quoted to her that the Bible says that "He will keep in perfect peace he whose mind is stayed on him." I told her, "I have thought of nothing else but Jesus from the time I realized my car had sped out of control and that I could do nothing. Jesus! Jesus! Jesus!" I would cry out with every bump, ever hit, every turnover, and every flip; than a big cry, 'JESUS' when the car landed upside down with a loud bang/crash.

A wonderful man from Carrizo Springs, Mauro Ybarra, helped me and called my husband, as he was the one who saw the most during the entire process of attempting to get me out of the car. It was the instruments from his truck that were used to break the windows and cut the seat belt. I pray that he, too, will come to Jesus and serve him after witnessing such a great dimension of God's loving care. When my husband arrived, he took the photo of my turned-over car that you see here.

I called a number in Carrizo that night and left a message that I would be testifying of God's miraculous sheltering arms, and that I would love him to be there. I told him I would like to publicly thank him before my family and my brothers and sisters in Christ. He was not able to attend, but I have had the privilege of seeing him twice after the accident to give him my thanks for being an instrument God used to save my life. A special thanks to all who came to my aid in that crucial hour --I do not know their names. God bless them all!

On the 40-minute ride in the ambulance to the Uvalde Memorial Hospital I began declaring to the beautiful ambulance attendee what God left me alive to declare. I told her, "Mi Hija (as we Hispanics lovingly call girls and young ladies), life is fragile and we are not guaranteed tomorrow. I made it, but what if I had not? I know I would be with Jesus, but what about you? Are you ready for eternity? I was flat on my back, but could sense from sobs I heard, that perhaps tears were wallowing up in her eyes, as she confessed her need to reflect on this. I remember asking, "Could it be that God allowed this so I could get in this ambulance and speak to you, one on one? How else would I ever have seen you and have such an opportunity to relate this message to you? We conversed all the way to Uvalde. She was so warm and created an atmosphere of tranquility. I felt such a love for her and continued to pray for her. I sensed God had great plans for this lovely gal and sent her as an extension of His hand to help me, while at the same time He used me to help her reflect and prepare for eternity.

Exams and X-rays followed and, to the glory of God, the tests showed no broken bones and no internal injuries. I had no scratches, no bruises, and no glass on my face nor body. I can only think that God kept me cradled up in a bubble of protection that nothing could penetrate.

I eventually learned her name was Lydia Tovar because on Mother's Day, about 3 weeks after the accident, she came to my home to wish me a Happy Mother's Day and to tell me that she was so glad I was alive. She mentioned that after witnessing the car smashed to the ground, the fire blazing high, and seeing all that had happened, and that I was so calm through it all, impacted her life. She told me it was only a miracle that I was alive. She saw the fence poles I hit down to the ground. She saw the telephone poles that were burned to about 20 feet high. Seventeen years later those telephone poles on Highway 83 still bear the black marks of being burned, a testament to God's divine protection and that I still have a purpose and assignment to fulfill in this life—to **PASS IT ON** and keep **PASSING IT ON** while I have the breath of life.

She mentioned that the words I shared with her on that trip to the hospital made her reflect on eternity and that she did ponder on everything I said. We prayed together and became close friends. She was a master seamstress and made amazing costumes. She would come over to share what she was making. Sadly, during

COVID she passed away. I was so sad and will miss her, but I was so glad I had met her, that I had the opportunity to pass on faith to her, and had the joy of establishing a friendship with her. Sometimes we think sharing our faith is from a pulpit, but it can be in an ambulance flat on your back, or in any setting where God opens up an opportunity.

LIFE IS FRAGILE, HANDLE WITH PRAYER

What lessons can you and I learn from this?

That life is fragile – handle it with devoted, intentional focused prayer

Be ready always for eternity. In the twinkling of an eye death can call our name or Jesus could come back to earth for His Church.

God's loving care can send angels to encompass us from fires that could blaze high as a result of the sparks that come when the vehicle of our lives crash into unexpected posts, brush, pavement, and fences no matter how high or strong those may be.

God's loving arms can keep us nestled close to him so that the broken-glass experiences of our lives and the debris of shattered heartbreaks won't cut us or leave bruises and abrasions. He specializes in the internal to secure that we will not have internal bleeding.

He can bring us out of any circumstance and turn it all for good, allowing us to proclaim His power, His love, His care, His Salvation—providing opportunities for us to **PASS IT ON!**

Always take advantage of the opportunities to say, "I love you" to those friends and loved ones when you are with them. Someday there may not be any more opportunities for you to express your love to them. Take time to make and leave treasured memories.

I have always said, "I will live my life pursuing the purposes for which He has given me life—to honor Him and to **PASS IT ON!** I will not hold back. I will not stop traveling if He ordains the trips. I will not stop preaching, teaching, sharing, giving, nor fulfilling the Great Commission. Hebrews 10:29 challenges me not to give up. *"**But we are not of those that shrink back and are destroyed, but of those who believe and are saved.**"*

So, the scripture I read that Monday morning was fulfilled in that, surrounded by fire, I was not burned nor did the flame scorch me. I had just filled up my car with gas, so it could have exploded, yet those words, "For I am the Lord, your God…your Savior." will resonate in my heart and my spirit as I continue to trust God. Let the words of this scripture speak hope and trust to your life as you read it, ponder on it, and try to memorize it: *"**Isaiah 43:2: When you pass through the water, I will be with you; and through the rivers, they shall not overflow you, for I am the Lord, your God. When you walk(go) through the fire, you shall not be burned,**"* *nor shall the flame scorch. For I am the Lord, your God, the Holy One of Israel, your Savior.*

So, if we are here, God has a plan and assignment for us: **PASS IT ON!**

PASS IT ON

The Baton of Service

The Mantle of Anointing

The Shield of Faith

The Torch of Pentecost

We are all leaving footprints.

May those who come behind us find us faithful.